"Dave Kraft has written a thorough and enlightening book on leadership that is easy to read and practical, full of great illustrations and stimulating quotations. This is a book for leaders who want to keep growing in their understanding of leadership, finish strongly, and lead with passion."

Mike Treneer, International President, The Navigators

"Drawing from three decades in ministry and coaching ministry leaders, my friend and fellow Mars Hill pastor Dave Kraft has combined his best insights into *Leaders Who Last*."

Mark Driscoll, Pastor of Mars Hill Church; President of Acts 29 and The Resurgence

"I love it when a practitioner, not a theorist, writes a book on leadership. I have known Dave for many years and his personal as well as his professional life is exemplary. He is someone you want to follow. He is a leader that knows how to last. He leads from conviction and character. He is a leader that understands how to place Christ at the center of his world and lead with purpose, passion, priorities, and proper pacing. *Leaders Who Last* is a powerful tool written by a respected leader who knows how to finish well."

Greg Salciccioli, Founding President of Ministry Coaching International

"*Leaders Who Last* is filled with practical principles to develop leaders who will influence others."

Scott Thomas, Director, Acts 29 Network

"This book carefully constructs a scriptural approach to leadership in a manner that is both accurate and practical. When you combine Dave's sound scriptural basis with his many years of successful leadership, you get a book that should become a handbook for Christians who are serious about learning to lead well. Christians at all levels of responsibility in their organizations will find this information invaluable to their personal growth and effective leadership."

Keith McGuire, Instructor at the University of Southern California's Aviation Safety Program

LEADERS
WHO LAST

Re:Lit Books

LEADERS
WHO LAST

....

Dave Kraft

WHEATON, ILLINOIS

Art direction and design: Patrick Mahoney of The Mahoney Design Team

First printing 2010

Printed in the United States of America

Trade paperback ISBN: 978-1-4335-1318-3

PDF ISBN: 978-1-4335-1319-0

Mobipocket ISBN: 978-1-4335-1320-6

ePub ISBN: 978-1-4335-2417-2

Library of Congress Cataloging-in-Publication Data
Kraft, Dave, 1939–
    Leaders who last / Dave Kraft ; foreword by Mark Driscoll.
        p. cm.
Includes bibliographical references.
    ISBN 978-1-4335-1318-3 (tpb)
    ISBN 978-1-4335-1319-0 — ISBN 978-1-4335-1320-6
    1. Leadership—Religious aspects—Christianity. I. Title.
BV4597.53.L43K73   2010
253—dc22   2009020444

Crossway is a publishing ministry of Good News Publishers.
VP   18   17   16   15   14   13
14   13   12   11   10   9   8

To

Roy Davis,

who significantly influenced me to become a Christian.

He also introduced me to The Navigators.

Roy has helped hundreds of people through the years,

and I am thankful to have been one of them.

And to

Warren Myers,

who passed away in April 2001.

Warren believed in me, encouraged me, mentored me,

and inspired me by modeling godly leadership.

Contents

Foreword

Pastor Dave Kraft is in the right season of life to write this book.

By the time this book is published he will be seventy years of age. On the month this book is released he will have been a Christian for fifty years, having been converted from a Jewish family. He has been in full-time ministry leadership for over forty years, both in parachurch ministries such as The Navigators, and churches such as Mars Hill where we pastor together. He has been faithfully married to the same woman for over forty years. He is both a father and a grandfather. He has coached, formally or informally, well over five hundred Christian leaders in both business and vocational ministry. He can still crush any twenty-year-old who is foolish enough to challenge him in racquetball (the list is impressively long). He expends all of his energies investing in Christian leaders, especially younger Christian leaders. And he does all of this while living with cancer and joyfully quoting Psalm 71:18: "So even to old age and gray hairs, O God, do not forsake me, until I proclaim your might to another generation, your power to all those to come."

In short, Pastor Dave Kraft is one of the few leaders who last.

He has helped me lead better and last longer. A few years back I was basically burned out in every way. The combination of the fast growth of our church, my lack of experience, and the immaturity of our organizational structures left me completely overextended. I was working out of my area of gifting, and it was literally breaking me, though I was only in my mid-thirties. My adrenal glands were fatigued. I could not sleep. I was seriously discouraged, exhausted, and frustrated.

At that time God brought into my life a handful of ministry and business leaders who were older, wiser, and humble enough to serve me. Pastor Dave Kraft was one of those men. As a professional ministry coach, he brought me through a formal coaching process and helped me get my life and ministry in better order. He gave me permission to make some very difficult decisions for the well-being of my family and our church. He wanted me to be one of the leaders who last.

A few years later, I can easily say I am in the best season of my life. The weight of ministry has not changed, but by God's grace, I keep changing. Now, I am glad to see a friend who served me well publish this book because we both want you to be one of the leaders who last. Sadly, too few Christian leaders finish well, and a combination of grace and wisdom cannot be overvalued. You will find both in this book.

I am deeply grateful for the investment that Pastor Dave Kraft has made in me and a long list of other leaders in Mars Hill Church, the Acts 29 church planting network, as well as other denominations, networks, and companies. I am also deeply grateful for the partnership we have at the Resurgence to publish Re:Lit with our friends and gospel partners at Crossway, and I want to thank Dave for writing this book and Crossway for publishing it. It is simple, helpful, practical, readable, and reliable.

Pastor Mark Driscoll
Preaching Pastor of Mars Hill Church
President of the Acts 29 Church
   Planting Network
President of The Resurgence

Acknowledgments

I have been the recipient of lots of help. The following individuals gave me ideas: Keith McGuire, Cheryl Meredith, Pete Pagan, Erick Goss, Pete Gerhard, Ron Bennett, and Adam Holtz. Louie Platt devoted many hours to proofreading and making needed corrections. Lastly, I want to thank author and church consultant Bill Easum, who first planted the seed in my heart to write a book on leadership.

Prologue

Bill Broadhurst entered a 10K race in Omaha, Nebraska. When he was younger, he suffered an aneurysm in the right side of his brain. It resulted in a partial paralysis on the left side of his body. Nonetheless, he was determined not only to enter but to finish the race because his hero, Bill Rogers (a world-class marathoner), would be in that race. Rogers won the race, finishing in twenty-nine minutes. It took Broadhurst two and a half hours. He was teased by children, became numb, experienced great pain, had to avoid cars (after they opened the race course up to traffic when they thought everyone had finished), and fought the desire to quit most of the way.

As the sun began to sink in the western Nebraska sky, Broadhurst could barely see the finish line. Approaching the end of the race, consuming the last fumes in his tank, Broadhurst saw Rogers suddenly step out of a darkened alley and welcome him, the partially paralyzed runner, as he stumbled across the line.

Rogers embraced him. Then he took the gold medal from around his own neck and placed it over Broadhurst's head, saying, "Broadhurst, you're the winner. Take the gold."[1]

Broadhurst finished the race. It was difficult and full of obstacles, but he made it to the end and received the gold medal from Rogers.

In 1 Corinthians 9:24–27 and 2 Timothy 4:7, Paul compares the Christian experience to a race. (The same comparison is also found in Hebrews 12:1–2.) The Christian journey is akin to a race—a marathon, not a short sprint. The key is not how you start the race, but how you finish it. Finishing well is what this book is all about.

Introduction

This book is about finishing your leadership race. It is a marathon, not a hundred-meter dash. Like Bill Broadhurst, you will encounter many obstacles and setbacks. But as a leader, your goal is to finish well—and not just to finish by yourself. You must aim to influence others so they can join you in your race and reach their fullest potential as they travel with you on your leadership journey.

The premise of this book is that you *can* learn how to be a good leader and finish your particular leadership race well. "Finishing well" can include (but is not limited to):

- maintaining a vibrant and rich walk with Jesus.
- having a solid relational network that includes at least one good friend with whom you can bare your soul.
- making a lasting and God-honoring contribution in your areas of passion and gifting.

My prayer and hope is that after reading this, you will have insight, motivation, discipline, and confidence. I trust that you will experience the grace of the Lord in such a way that, at the end of your journey, you will hear the Lord say, "Well done, good and faithful servant."

Why is this topic so close to my heart? So many leaders are not doing well and are ending up shipwrecked. Professor Bobby Clinton at Fuller Seminary in Pasadena, California, is a key spokesperson on the subject of leadership within the body of Christ. His landmark book, *The Making of a Leader*, is a must-read for those in leadership positions.[1] Clinton has come to the conclusion that only 30 percent of leaders finish well. That is deeply disturbing.

There are many things that prevent us from finishing well in this crazy, fast-paced world. Leaders fight battles within and without that cause them to plateau, quit, or be disqualified. As I lead others, study the subject of leadership, and coach emerging leaders, I admit that I am deeply concerned. Too many are dropping out of the race, losing heart, and letting go of their dreams and lofty purposes. They are simply giving up and throwing in the towel. Due to the rapidly changing and fast-paced world we live in, it is increasingly difficult to lead and lead well with joy, clarity, and confidence. Some just hang on by their fingernails, waiting for retirement to rescue them from their disappointments, fears, and frustrations. What will it take for you and me to be leaders who finish the race well? What issues should we be aware of that could hold us back and keep us from finishing?

I read everything I can get my hands on that deals with the subject of leadership, and I am inclined to agree with some who believe that everything rises or falls on leadership. Without the right kind of leaders, organizations seldom go anywhere and the people who lead them fall short of their true potential. Without the right kind of leaders, organizations become bloated bureaucracies concerned more with policy, politics, and procedures than with creativity and innovation. Sooner or later they have the life choked out of them and quickly become an endangered species!

Most of the leadership books in my library are based on surveys and studies that attempt to crystallize key principles and proven methodologies for discovering, developing, and deploying leaders. These books are written by successful CEOs of large organizations or professors in MBA programs who use the business world as their model.

In contrast, this book is written from my personal leadership journey of over forty years. It is not the result of interviews and surveys from the business sector, nor is it the product of analyzing and dissecting successful leaders from the Bible or history. Instead, it is a personal and extremely practical account of essential leadership principles I have learned and use. As a simple, down-to-earth guide to Christian leadership, this book was born out of leading, teaching leadership, and personally coaching dozens of Christian leaders. It is an easy-to-understand road map for leadership, because I am an active practitioner, not an academic theorist. Everything in this book flows from my personal experience and convictions.

Leaders Who Last is written from a Christian perspective. As I write, my words are primarily, but not exclusively, addressed to the following types of church leaders:

- Senior pastors
- Ministry staff members
- Volunteer leaders

- Sunday school teachers
- Small-group leaders
- Leaders in local parachurch organizations

I love the church. There is nothing as exciting as the local church when it is properly and dynamically led by the right kinds of leaders. I became a follower of Jesus Christ through the ministry of a local church and ever since have had a burden for local churches.

I share Paul's sentiment expressed in 2 Corinthians 11:28: "There is the daily pressure on me of my anxiety for all the churches." There are many things to be concerned about today in the church scene:

- A multitude of churches have plateaued, are dying, or are already dead.
- Antiquated forms and methods that no longer work are still in use today.
- Worship wars are raging.
- There is a lack of deep spirituality among church members.
- There is an absence of intentional and relevant outreach.

But my biggest concern is the lack of the right kind of leadership. I have a deep and abiding concern for leaders in local churches. This book is an attempt to address all these concerns.

If you are currently in a leadership position or anticipate that you will be in the near future, it should become increasingly clear to you that you will need to live and lead in a new way. This is necessary to stay viable as a leader, survive your journey, and accomplish your objective.

Times have changed, the culture has changed, rules have changed, and expectations of leaders have changed. metathesiophobia is the impossible-to-pronounce word for "fear of change." Fearing, resisting, or balking at the need to change, grow, and adapt can be your undoing as a leader. It can start a downward spiral for your organization or group. The only thing that seems to remain the same is change. Change is more prolific, rapid, and complex than ever before. The only place you can't be sure of change is from a vending machine. Everything else is up for grabs.

Here are a few obvious contrasts in the way we need to lead today compared to the ways we've led in the past.

Past Leaders	Future Leaders
Organizational	Relational
Operate in committees	Operate in teams
Command and control	Permission-giving
Degreed and elected	Gifted and called
Linear and pyramidal	Overlapping circles
Share propositional truth	Tell stories
People of the written page	People of the screen
Tightly structured	Highly flexible
Emphasize position	Emphasize empowerment

My desire is that sharing my experience will provide ideas that will aid you as a leader. I also hope to help you build into the lives of those you lead. How will you find newer and younger leaders for the next generation, and what will you need to do with them and for them so that they finish well?

Let's begin by defining our terms. People use the word

"leader" in a variety of ways. Some thinkers and writers are of the opinion that everybody is a leader because we all influence people in one way or another. At the opposite end of the spectrum are those who define leader so rigidly and exhaustively that even Jesus wouldn't qualify. Their list of essential qualities and ingredients is endless and overwhelming.

I have sought to understand and then define what experience has taught me about the nature of leadership. At the moment, I am in between the two extremes of "everybody is a leader" and "a leader as the fourth person of the Trinity" (i.e., a leader who thinks he is a super-leader—omniscient and omnipotent, like the Father, Son, and Holy Spirit).

Before I toss my current working definition of "leader" on the table, allow me to share a deep conviction. The greatest and most pressing need in the body of Christ today is an army of leaders who have a vision of a desired future and are called and anointed by God. These leaders possess a fire burning in their hearts that can't be extinguished. They are motivated and led by God to intentionally, passionately, and effectively influence others.

Local churches are well populated with leaders who are good teachers, sensitive counselors, and detailed administrators. These roles and functions are necessary. But we need much more than that—oh, so much more! We desperately need visionary leaders like Paul, who said to Agrippa, "I was not disobedient to the heavenly vision" (Acts 26:19). Most organizations are over-managed and under-led. That needs to change or the body of Christ will be in deep trouble.

Here is how I define "leader" throughout this book:

A Christian leader is a humble, God-dependent, team-playing servant of God who is called by God to shepherd, develop, equip, and empower a specific group of believers to accomplish an agreed-upon vision from God.

These are the key ingredients of leadership:

- Christian leaders are, first and foremost, servants (bond slaves) of the Lord, and second, servants of those they are leading.
- They are characterized by humility, dependence, and team-playing, rather than being a loner or one-man show.
- Christian leaders are called by God into leadership. They do not decide for themselves to be a leader. They are not pushed into leadership by well-meaning supporters, nor do they arrive at leadership because no one else will do it.
- Christian leaders have at least four major responsibilities:
    - *Shepherding*—a leader loves and cares for those being led.
    - *Developing*—a leader helps those being led in their personal walk with Jesus Christ to become fully devoted followers.
    - *Equipping*—a leader trains those being led for ministry.
    - *Empowering*—a leader inspires, encourages, affirms, believes in, and frees people up to serve out of their gifting.
- Christian leaders are moving toward a specific destination.
- Christian leaders are creating and sustaining an agreed-upon vision. There is an initial buy-in and a growing ownership of the vision among those being led.

I promise you an interesting and worthwhile trip. Let the race begin!

Foundations

Because leading is a reflection of who you are, you lead from the inside out. The leader must live in five areas (as demonstrated by the center hub and four spokes of the leadership wheel):

- With Jesus Christ in the center as your *power*
- With Jesus Christ as you develop a *purpose*
- With Jesus Christ as you develop a *passion*
- With Jesus Christ as you set *priorities*
- With Jesus Christ as you develop *pacing* for how much you accomplish and how fast you do it

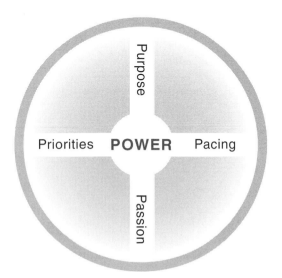

CHAPTER 1:

The Leader's Power

*"Remember that the power comes through you,
not from you."*

FRED SMITH SR.

POWER

As a leader, everything I am and everything I do needs to be anchored in my identity with Christ. Leadership begins and ends with a clear understanding of the gospel and being rooted in the grace of Jesus Christ as a free gift.

Gospel Identity

I am saved and kept by the power of God and am a Christian and a leader by grace and grace alone. I didn't earn it and I don't deserve it. Ephesians 2:8–9 says it well: "For by grace you have been saved through faith. And this is not your own doing; it is the gift of God, not a result of works, so that no one may boast." As I lead, I lead out of the reality of being saved by Jesus, and Jesus alone, and empowered by the Holy Spirit for the leadership role and responsibilities to which he calls me. It is too easy for the work and the ministry to be the center instead of Jesus himself.

I had a rude awakening a few years ago. I was asked to speak to a group of pastors at a retreat on the subject of the pastor's personal devotional life. As we launched into the first day, I was shocked to find out that most of the pastors only spent time with the Lord in his Word when preparing for preaching and teaching. I thought this was highly unusual, since I was taught early how important it is to feed myself from Scripture before seeking to give spiritual sustenance to others. Ezra 7:10 has long been my benchmark: "For Ezra had set his heart to study the Law of the LORD, and to do it and to teach his statutes and rules in Israel." First, I study and apply God's Word to my life. Then I teach others.

Since that retreat, I have discovered that many leaders have never established spiritual habits of the heart that include confession and worship, as well as intake of the Word of God. This is vital to staying connected with Jesus, the power source of our life and ministry.

In order to achieve balance in my life as a Christian leader (and yes, I believe it is possible), I start with Jesus Christ in the center. Jesus Christ is my power. I desire to tap into his infinite energy daily and consistently and to not rely on my own finite power supply.

Spiritual Disciplines

I realize that different leaders use different methods and tools to help them accomplish that balance and to stay fresh and vibrant in their walk with God. In many cases, this is accomplished through Christian disciplines.

Some of these disciplines are:

- The study of Scripture
- Spending time in prayer and worship
- Taking time for extended periods of solitude, meditation, and fasting

These disciplines create a state of mind that is receptive to the grace of God that keeps us fresh in our personal relationship with the Lord Jesus Christ.

My Christian life began by experiencing Jesus as my Savior from the penalty of sin, and embracing his death on the cross for myself. I responded to his gracious invitation to come to him. At twenty years of age, I acknowledged that I had sinned, repented of my sin, and accepted Jesus' offer to be part of his family. From that point on I have gradually learned how to walk with him and stay in close contact with him through the practice of some well-tested disciplines (or "holy habits of the heart").

Motorboats, Sailboats, and Rafts

The following thoughts from John Ortberg are insightful:

One of the analogies that's been kind of helpful to me is the difference between a motorboat, a raft, and a sailboat. In a motorboat, I'm in charge. I determine how fast we're going to go, and in what direction. Some people approach spiritual disciplines that way. If I'm just aggressive enough, if I have enough quiet times, I can make transformation happen on my own.

Some people have been burned by that kind of approach, so they go to the opposite extreme and will say, "I'm into grace." It's like they're floating on a raft. If you ask them to do anything to further their growth, they'll say, "Hey, no. I'm not into works. I'm into grace. You're getting legalistic with me." So they drift. There are way too many commands in Scripture for anybody to think that we're called to be passive.

On a sailboat, however, I don't move if it's not for the wind. I can't control the wind. I don't manufacture the wind. Jesus talks about the Spirit blowing like the wind. But there is a role for me to play, and part of it has to do with what I need to discern. A good sailor will discern, *Where's the wind at work? How should I set the sails?* Practicing spiritual disciplines is like sailing.[1]

It is vitally important that each of us discovers his own pathway to deep intimacy with the Lord Jesus Christ. For some, the way is music. For others, it is through thinking and reflection. Others find intimacy by observing and enjoying God's creation, and still others when they experience authentic community. I try to use a combination of things, such as prayer walks, personal retreats, a daily devotional time, worshipful music, genuine community, or accountability with close and honest friends.

My Spiritual Disciplines

Allow me to specifically share some of my holy habits of the heart with you. These practices consistently tap into the power of Jesus to sustain me and flow through my life as a leader. Take these and adapt them in such a way that they nourish you and stretch your soul.

When I awake in the morning, I roll out of bed, fall on my knees, and silently (in my spirit and as a prayer) run through a little song: "Fill me, fill me, fill me through and through. Fill me, fill me. Make me more like you. Fill me up, O Lord, today. Have your will, and have your way."

It is my deepest desire to put God in the driver's seat in my first waking moments; not my agenda but his, not my energy but his, not my will but his. I desperately want that—and need that—if I am going to experience the joy of the Lord.

I then go downstairs to spend time in Scripture reading, study, meditation, and prayer. I am very thankful that when I first became a believer, a few people encouraged me to spend daily time with the Lord by reading Scripture and praying.

My time through the years has varied, changed, and grown, but two ingredients have remained the same: I read and absorb God's Word, and then I pray, seeking to respond to what he has shown me from the Word. I confess, thank, praise, pray for others, and share my heart, my fears, my desires, and my frustrations with "the blessed and only Sovereign" (1 Tim. 6:15).

In my Bible reading, I practice the "Four R's":

1. *Read.* Reading and marking the words and verses that speak to me.
2. *Reflect.* Thinking about what I have marked.
3. *Respond.* Focusing on truths I marked to pray about and obey.
4. *Record.* Capturing what God has said in writing (a journal).

The "Four R's" set the stage for God to whisper in my ear, tell me he loves me, guide me in important issues and decisions, and confront sin in its various and often subtle manifestations. I still see that my heart is deceitful and desperately sick (Jer. 17:9), and I am an expert at rationalizing and trying to kid myself into believing that my sin is not sin.

During my time alone with the Lord, I am worshipful and contrite in his presence. I genuinely want to hear from him and experience him. I ask him to search my heart to see if there is any sin I need to deal with (Ps. 51:10; 139:23–24). I want to open myself up and exchange who I am for who I can become. I want to exchange my sinfulness for his righteousness. I want to exchange my fears for his confidence.

Over the years I have learned that:

- When my times alone with the Savior are missing or inconsistent, genuine enthusiasm and purpose give way to "grinding out the work of ministry" with an accompanying loss of joy.
- As I experience intimacy with the Lord, I find myself living life from a solid, integrated sense of purpose that taps into the power of God.
- My time with God is about developing a relationship, not about fulfilling obligations or checking items off my to-do list.
- Great men and women of God are great because they enjoy exceptional intimacy with the Lord. The failure to establish intimacy imposes a limit on genuine spiritual development and effectiveness.

Discipline or Legalism

Because I tend to be very disciplined and structured, I need to be careful that these regular holy habits don't degenerate into an empty pharisaical system of earning favor. Author Dallas Willard observed that "grace is not opposed to effort, but to earning." That means that it is not wrong to expend energy and effort to get to know the Lord, but it is unbiblical to do so with the thought of earning God's love, favor, and acceptance through the effort.

My standing with Jesus is not based on what I do, but on what he has done; not on my works, but on his free gift (Eph. 2:8–10). Effort definitely has a place in the Christian experience, but it is a result of salvation, not a means to salvation.

Sometimes it is difficult for me to make the distinction between effort and earning. I can easily fall into the trap of thinking that God loves me more or thinks more highly of me when I am faithful in my holy habits. It can become like school with all its rules and regulations. I want to be disciplined but not legalistic. I want to be grace-based, not rule-based.

I ran across the following that helps me have joy in my spiritual habits and avoid the pitfalls of my structured and systematic nature:

I will delight in your statutes. (Ps. 119:16)

It seems almost too simple, doesn't it? Naïve. At best, it sounds old-fashioned and quaint. Who comes to the Word of God with delight anymore? Aren't we more sophisticated than that today?

We come with determination, diligence, discipline, and a sense of duty.

We bring charts, commentaries, concordances, dictionaries, encyclopedias, guides, graphs, maps, outlines, schedules, summaries, systems, and study helps.

We search for applications, attitudes, comparisons, concepts, contrasts, commands, cross-references, examples, exhortations, illustrations, repetitions, statistics, and warnings.

We discover key words, key verses, key thoughts, key statements, and key chapters.

Foundations

We develop word studies, topical studies, character studies, and prayer studies.

We use translations, paraphrases, versions, and revisions of versions.

We read and reread until we become well-versed.

We are experts on Bible-study methods.

What could the psalmist have been thinking of when he said, "I will delight in your statutes"? Surely, this approach is too childish for mature Bible students! Still, some of us wonder, "Do you suppose it would be all right with the Father if we were to sort of ditch school once in a while and just curl up with a good book? It really is delightful." [2]

So, the power-tapping idea begins for me on my knees, as I surrender my day to the Lord. It then progresses as I spend time with the Lord in the Word and prayer. With his help, I carry that spirit and attitude throughout the day. I confess when I step out on my own, and rejoice when he gently nudges and reminds me that he wants to be my power supply. He guides me back to the source: himself!

John 15 is a great chapter on abiding in Christ. There is a deep and constant longing in my heart to experience genuine, intimate dependency on God on an ongoing basis. I get so tired so fast and stay tired longer when I fall into the trap of believing it's all up to me.

I have enjoyed Eugene Peterson's interpretive comments on Matthew 11:28–30: "Walk with me and work with me—watch how I do it. Learn the unforced rhythms of grace. I won't lay anything heavy or ill-fitting on you. Keep company with me and you'll learn to live freely and lightly" (MESSAGE). I just love that!

For me it creates a mental picture of what it means to walk with the Lord Jesus Christ on a moment-by-moment basis. I especially like his thought, "Learn the unforced rhythms of grace." This encourages me to think that it can be learned, that I personally can learn it, and that the Lord *wants* me to learn it.

I see in my mind a surfer effortlessly riding a wave as he moves up and down in sync with the powerful surge of the changing waves. I imagine a horseback rider moving in sync with the horse. I sense after my many years of rigidity that this "learning the unforced rhythms of grace" constitutes the starting point for fruitful, joyful living and ministry.

The remaining spokes in the wheel have their roots in Jesus as the source of power. You will not have purpose, passion, priorities, or pacing if you're trying to achieve it on your own. "Not by might, nor by power, but by my Spirit, says the LORD" (Zech. 4:6). Flowing out of a Christ-centered power, you are ready to discover his unique purpose for your life.

CHAPTER 2

The Leader's Purpose

"A leader is a person with a magnet in his heart and a compass in his head."

ROBERT TOWNSEND

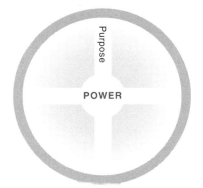

My supervisor, Jim Downing, sat across from me in my living room in Stockholm, Sweden, in the late '70s. I was frustrated with both the lack of direction and the lack of fruit in my life. I poured my soul out to him. "So," he asked, "If you could do anything, what would you want to do?"

I thought for a moment and then said, "Jim, this might sound strange, but I'm not sure I have an answer to that question. I should have some clarity on such an important issue. But I don't. I just don't. I am thirty-eight years old, but I can honestly say I have never thought about what I really want to do."

At that point I had been on staff with The Navigators for ten years. For the last several years I had been experiencing a lack of motivation, uncertainty, and no clear direction or joy in my assignment as a missionary to Sweden. Something was missing, but I wasn't sure what it was. "Well," Jim continued, "give it some thought and prayer, and let me know when you have an answer."

Searching for Answers

I felt a keen sense of disappointment. I was a mature Christian involved in full-time ministry and I didn't have a clue about my purpose, calling, or direction. I didn't even have an answer to Jim's simple question: "What would you like to do?"

After I recovered from the confusion and disappointment with myself, I sensed the need to get away for a few days to pray, fast, and think things through. I really wanted to get a handle on what my life's purpose was. I borrowed the upper floor of a friend's home and hid away for three days to wrestle in prayer with the Lord. I took my Bible, a legal pad, a couple of books, and most importantly, a strong determination not to leave that room until I had some sense of direction.

This was a watershed experience for me. I won't go into all the details except to say that I developed a list of things I should be doing that would truly be an expression of the man the Lord made me to be. This became a launching pad that enabled me to later move into a role that truly matched the person I was. My family and I eventually left Sweden and returned to the United States.

Over time, a strong sense of purpose began to emerge. The crowning moment took place on my old high school campus.

Epiphany

I was in Sue Krenwinkle's office (the high school counselor for my four children) with one of my daughters. As we were discussing an issue, a collage on the wall behind Sue's desk transfixed me. There were dozens of pictures of her students at football games, school outings, proms, etc. Right in the middle of it all was a quote, which is now displayed on my desk at home:

> Some people come into our lives and quietly go. Others stay awhile, and leave footprints on our hearts, and we are never the same.

I lost track of the conversation we were having. I lost track of time. I lost track of everything. I was mesmerized by that quote. "What an incredible thought," I whispered under my breath. "Lord," I prayed softly in my heart, "make me a person who leaves footprints in people's lives. I don't want to be a person who comes and goes with no lasting impact. Because of contact with me, may people never be the same again. May I be a person who intentionally and lastingly influences others." As that prayer flooded my heart and mind, the process gave birth to my purpose statement, which I wrote down a short time later:

> To leave footprints in the hearts of God-hungry leaders who multiply.

My Purpose

It is clear to me that I was designed to be in the leader-development business. I mentor, coach, and invest in the next generation of leaders. That is my purpose, my unique contribution to the body of Christ and the kingdom of God.

I want to leave footprints in the lives of people—not just any person, but leaders and influencers who are hungry for God. Many leaders I encounter are self-satisfied. They think they know enough. They aren't hungry or thirsty for more of God, more growth, and more fruitfulness.

I will not invest my time in them.

Some are hungry, but just for themselves with no intention of reproducing anything in the lives of others.

I will not invest in them.

I am looking for God-hungry leaders who are dissatisfied

with the status quo (Latin for "the mess we are in"). I am looking for leaders who want to move on in their lives, move out in faith, and move up to their true God-given potential. It's now so clear to me who I am and what I am about. My purpose focuses me like a laser beam. I am like a ray of sunshine that, when captured through a magnifying glass, has great power and intensity.

I am motivated by the words of Rudyard Kipling who wrote in his poem "L'Envoi" of the artists in heaven:

> And only the Master shall praise us,
> and only the Master shall blame;
> And no one shall work for money,
> and no one shall work for fame;
> But each for the joy of the working,
> and each in his separate star,
> Shall draw the Thing as he sees It
> for the God of the Things as They Are![1]

With a clear sense of purpose, I can "draw the thing" as I see it for the "God of the things as they are." Otherwise, my drawings may be random scribbles, with no end in view.

There is a story about a bank president who retired. Before his retirement, this gentleman had a morning routine that mystified his employees. First thing each morning, he would walk to his desk, take a key out of his coat pocket, open a small drawer in his desk, look in it for a couple of seconds, and then lock it and begin his duties.

The Monday morning after the retirement party, the new president quickly went to the prior president's desk. With all the employees gathered around, he took the key and opened the secret drawer. In that drawer was a small note with the words, "Credits to the right, debits to the left."

The guiding principle for the bank president's work was basic, simple, and foundational. That is what my purpose statement should be for me. I want it to be the first thing I think about in the morning and the last thing I think about at night. It is the due north on the compass of my life.

Once I have a clear sense of purpose flowing out of my relationship with the Lord Jesus Christ, it is amazing how instrumental this purpose is in managing the day-to-day details of my life—the decisions I make, the people I spend time with, and the books I read. I am slowly but surely experiencing that most of what I do flows out of my purpose statement.

The following notice appeared in the window of a coat store in Nottingham, England:

> We have been established for over 100 years and have been pleasing and displeasing customers ever since. We have made money and lost money, suffered the effects of coal nationalization, coal rationing, government control, and bad payers. We have been cussed and discussed, messed about, lied to, held up, robbed, and swindled. The only reason we stay in business is to see what happens next.

Why are you and I in business? What is our purpose?

Most successful enterprises, both private and public, have some sort of purpose or mission statement. It helps the leaders make decisions and prioritize activities, and—coupled with a vision for the future and a set of core values—keeps them on task with a high degree of morale and enthusiasm. I now have a purpose for my life that accomplishes the same for me.

Your Life's Purpose Statement

Do you have a brief purpose statement for your life? Peter Drucker says it should be short enough to put on a T-shirt. It should give you energy, motivation, and direction. Do you have clarity about the fulfillment of your dream, the accomplishment of your task, and the completion of your race? Do you want to finish well? Remember that according to Bobby Clinton, only 30 percent of leaders finish well.[2]

Having a biblically based purpose is like holding a magnet. It motivates, directs, and pulls you around detours and through distractions. If your activities flow out of a God-given purpose and are anchored in a Christ-centered power, you will have a reliable road map for your life.

Scripture Speaks of Purpose

As I read the Gospels and Paul's letters, it seems clear there was a compelling purpose that guided Jesus and Paul, like an internal gyroscope. Jesus speaks of this in John 17:4, where he says, "I glorified you on earth, having accomplished the work that you gave me to do."

Jesus had two purposes for his earthly life: to die for the sins of the world, and to train twelve disciples to carry on his ministry of evangelism and discipleship. His purpose was clear and he stayed on track throughout his life and ministry.

Similarly, Paul speaks of his own life in Acts 20:24: "But I do not account my life of any value nor as precious to myself, if only

I may finish my course and the ministry that I received from the Lord Jesus." At the end of his life he could say with confidence, "I have fought the good fight, I have finished the race, I have kept the faith" (2 Tim. 4:7).

One of the best books I have found on the subject of formulating your purpose is *The Path* by Laurie Beth Jones.[3] I once read this fantastic quote by Jones: "A purpose statement is, in essence, a written-down reason for being. Jesus' mission helped him decide how to act, what to do, and even what to say when challenging situations arose. Clarity is power: Once you are clear about what you were put here to do then 'jobs' become only a means toward accomplishing your mission, not an end in themselves."

The Unhappy Businessman Who Had It All

Os Guinness records this sobering confession by a successful businessman with no clear purpose:

"As you know, I have been very fortunate in my career and I've made a lot of money—far more than I ever dreamed of. Far more than I could ever spend, far more than my family needs." The speaker was a prominent businessman at a conference near Oxford University. The strength of his determination and character showed in his face, but a moment's hesitation betrayed deeper emotions hidden behind the outward intensity. A single tear rolled slowly down his well-tanned cheek. "To be honest, one of my motives for making so much money was simple—to have the money to hire people to do what I don't like doing.

"But there's one thing I've never been able to hire anyone to do for me: find my own sense of purpose and fulfillment. I'd give anything to discover that."[4]

Foundations

My deep desire would be to sit down with that wealthy, directionless man and give him some practical steps to discover his true purpose in life. I long for the same thing for those reading this book. Words cannot adequately or effectively communicate what a difference a compelling purpose has had in my life. Here are a few steps that will help you on the road to identifying your purpose:

1. Record Bible passages God has applied to your life.
2. Reflect on how God has used you in the past.
3. Determine what you are passionate about.
4. List your known gifts and strengths.
5. Delineate what you have excelled at in your work experience.
6. Define what action words best describe what you like to do.
7. Write down what you enjoy doing in your free time.
8. Reread all your answers.
9. Take note of common themes.
10. Write down key words or ideas that repeat.
11. Summarize those key words in a short, energizing statement about yourself.

Purpose and Career

I have come to the conclusion that it is easy to confuse purpose and career. When I speak of a compelling purpose, I am speaking about the spiritual focus of your life. Whatever your career may be—teacher, chemical engineer, pastor, doctor, lawyer, janitor— you have a purpose that is higher and more eternally significant than what you do to put bread on the table.

I once read, "People today are talking about calling, vocation, and destiny more than ever. A *USA Today* poll discovered that if most people could ask God one question, it would be: 'What's my purpose in life?'"[5]

What is your God-given purpose? Have you identified it? What has the Lord gifted and called you to do in the body of Christ and among the lost? What is your contribution to the Great Commandment and the Great Commission? It so happens that I am a pastor and the director of Coaching and Leadership Development for the Resurgence Training Center at Mars Hill Church in Seattle. That is my career. But my purpose (in the context of my career) is to discover, develop, and deploy God-hungry leaders.

I would be doing that if I were a doctor, engineer, public school teacher, or anything else.

I would always be on the lookout for those special people in whom God would want me to invest—some during the working hours of my career, and some during the nonworking hours, evenings, or weekends. It all begins with keeping Jesus Christ central through the practice of time-proven discipline (holy habits of the heart). Out of that relationship with him, a clear purpose is crafted. It is based on who he created me to be and how he has gifted me.

When you are plugged into Jesus and have a clear, defined purpose, it will create a sense of joy and enthusiasm in your leadership role and responsibilities.

CHAPTER 3

The Leader's Passion

"The most powerful weapon on earth is the human soul on fire."

FIELD MARSHAL FERDINAND FOCH

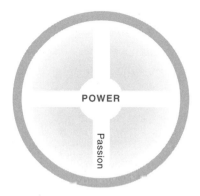

I once read a book written by Bill Bradley, senator and former NBA star. Bradley related a story of a gentleman who approached him after a game and asked Bradley if he really loved to play basketball. Bradley replied that there was nothing he would rather be doing at this point in his life than play basketball. The man remarked that he had once felt that same way about playing the trumpet in a little band he led in high school. His dad, however, squelched the idea by telling his son that he had no future playing in a band. So he stopped playing, and later went on to law school. Bradley asked him how it was being a lawyer. The man replied rather matter-of-factly that it was OK, and then quickly added, "but nothing like playing the trumpet."[1]

This man was making a living, but not living a life that had passion and excitement. He probably would have been better off in the long run if he had stayed with the trumpet, making less money but loving what he did.

When President Kennedy was thinking about his life direction, a friend gave him some good advice:

> Plan your life, as you want it. . . . Go up the steps of fame. But—
> pause now and then to make sure that you are accompanied by
> happiness. Stop and ask yourself *"Does it sing inside me today."*
> If that is gone, look around and don't take another step till you
> are certain life is as you will and want it.[2] (emphasis added)

It is very important that what I do is a reflection of my life purpose—that this purpose sings inside me today, that I am playing my own "trumpet." There is entirely too much passion-less living and working today. I, for one, am through with it.

The Importance of Passion

Passion is contagious. Passion will have more of an impact than personality. There is something compelling about leaders who love what they do and do what they love. A leader like this has the power to ignite enthusiasm and dedication in scores of others with whom he has contact. Life is too short to be boring or medio-cre. I am one who has always respected, admired, and looked up to leaders with contagious and infectious passion.

I lived in Colorado Springs from 1984 to 1988 and had the privilege of knowing Bill Retts. At the time, Bill was in his mid-eighties. He had more passion and enthusiasm than any person I ever met. Bill took me under his wing and became my mentor during the time we were in Toastmasters together. He modeled passion and taught me how to speak and live with a passion that came from deep within.

At eighty, Bill continued putting together presentations and traveling around the world, speaking, teaching, and mentor-ing younger men like me. Passion oozed from every pore in his excited, positive, energetic body. He loved the Lord, he loved his work, and he loved people. He was excited and delighted to be alive, and it was obvious to everybody. I thank the Lord for bringing Bill Retts into my life.

I love to be around people of passion. Most people do. I am not talking about a phony enthusiasm and hype that is manufactured to sell things or persuade people to get on board with a novel idea. I'm referring to a genuine joy that flows from a leader in love with Jesus Christ, one who has a compelling purpose that ignites a deep inner passion.

Another Bill is Microsoft founder Bill Gates, one of the world's wealthiest men. He says that what he does best is share his enthusiasm. Some may contend that what he does best is make money. But one of the main reasons he makes so much is that he is truly passionate about his company, its products, and its vision.

I live in Seattle, the home of Microsoft, and I know people who work for Mr. Gates. They tell me it is an exhilarating place to work. There is joy, excitement, and expectancy in the air that is truly contagious. People all over the world are on waiting lists to work for Microsoft.

I recall hearing about two pastors who were discussing their theological positions when one said to the other, "Well, it appears to me that we basically believe the same things."

The other responded, "Yes, but the difference is that you have it on ice and we have it on fire."

I have met many leaders during my forty years of ministry who teach the truth on ice. The facts are there, the doctrines are biblical, but they are served on ice. There is no life, no joy, no burning heart, and no God-fueled passion.

D. L. Moody was once asked how he had become the engaging, passionate communicator that he was. He responded by saying that before he was to speak, he would go out into a field by himself and ask God to set him on fire. Think what would happen if leaders began praying to be set on fire. I have started to pray that for myself.

We need more of this kind of passion. There's too little fire and too much ice that coats much of what goes on today in the name of Christ.

Edward G. E. Bulwer-Lytton said, "Nothing is so contagious as enthusiasm. It is the genius of sincerity, and truth accomplishes no victories without it." And I have heard John Maxwell say that passion will enable you to:

- believe things you never would have believed.
- feel things you never would have felt.
- attempt things you never would have attempted.
- accomplish things you never would have accomplished.
- meet people you otherwise would not have met.
- motivate people you never would have motivated.[3]

Passion and Personality

Now, I suspect that some of you who are on the quiet side may be tempted to brush aside this encouragement to be passionate. You might categorize passion as the personality trait of charismatic, outgoing, somewhat loony, naturally energetic people. Before you go too far down that road, let me tell you that I am introverted by nature, but I am as passionate as they come.

Passion is a God thing, not a personality thing. The Lord wants all his leaders to be so in love with him, so excited about his purpose for their lives, that a deep, heartfelt passion results. Granted, that will look different for a quiet leader than for an outgoing leader (and so it should!).

The passion displayed by Peter is different from that of his brother, Andrew. Paul had a different personality than Timothy. Timothy may have been on the timid side (2 Tim. 1:7), but was nonetheless encouraged by Paul to be passionate. And so it is throughout the Bible: different Christian leaders have different combinations of gifts and different personalities, but all are passionate because they are deeply connected with God and his purpose for their lives.

Keep in mind that passion is a God thing, something that the Spirit of God creates in our hearts as a result of our deep convictions about who he is and who we are in him. Nevertheless, there are some steps we can take to develop genuine and contagious passion:

1. Pray like Moody did for God to set you on fire. Ask him to give you passion within the context of how he has designed you.
2. Listen to CDs and read books by passionate, on-fire servants of God.
3. Choose to spend time around passionate people. There is power in association. "Whoever walks with the wise becomes wise, but the companion of fools will suffer harm" (Prov. 13:20). Those who hang out with people of passion

will acquire passion. You can't spend time around people with fire in their souls without having it ignite you. (That is why I spent all the time I could with Bill Retts, for example.)

4. Attend seminars or conferences that will give you solid teaching on developing convictions, fire, and passion. Sometimes I will listen to speakers not only for the content, but also so that I can drink deeply from their passion. Remember, passion is a God thing, not a personality thing.

Setting the Bar High

I ran across the following letter written by a young Communist to his fiancée, breaking off their engagement.

We Communists have a high casualty rate. We are the ones who get shot and hung and ridiculed and fired from our jobs and in every other way made as uncomfortable as possible.

A certain percentage of us get killed or imprisoned. We live in virtual poverty. We turn back to the Party every penny we make above what is absolutely necessary to keep us alive.

We Communists do not have the time or the money for movies, concerts, T-bone steaks, decent homes, or new cars. We have been described as fanatics. We are fanatics. Our lives are dominated by one great overshadowing factor: the struggle for world communism. We Communists have a philosophy of life, which no amount of money can buy. We have a cause to fight for, a definite purpose in life. We subordinate our petty personal selves to a great movement of humanity.

And if our personal lives seem hard or our egos appear to suffer through subordination to the Party, then we are adequately compensated by the thought that each of us in his small way is contributing to something new and true and better for mankind.

There is one thing that I am in dead earnest about, and that is the Communist cause. It is my life, my business, my religion, my hobby, my sweetheart, my wife, my mistress, and my bread and meat. I work at it in the daytime and dream of it at night. Its hold on me grows, not lessens as time goes on. Therefore, I cannot carry on a friendship, a love affair, or even a conversation without relating it to this force which both drives and guides my life. I evaluate people, books, ideas, and actions according to how they affect the Communist cause, and by their attitude toward it. I've already been in jail because of my ideals, and if necessary, I'm ready to go before a firing squad.[4]

Now that's passion! I can only imagine what it would look like if that kind of attitude permeated Christian leaders today.

When I read the book of Acts, that's what I see: boldness, fire, fearlessness, and convictions worth dying for; not obsession with safety or comfort, but pure, unadulterated love for Jesus and for the vision he left with us. Passion needs to be recaptured in all its fullness within the ranks of Christian leadership. Away with the ice! Bring on the fire that consumes, burns away the dross, and gives light and life to a dying world.

There are two additional and essential ingredients in our leadership wheel: priorities and pacing. The presence of these will greatly help us, but their absence will greatly hinder and harm us in living out the power, purpose, and passion for which we were designed. We will address these ingredients in the following two chapters.

CHAPTER 4

The Leader's Priorities

"Opportunity doesn't equal obligation."

ANDY STANLEY

Priorities   POWER

I attended a conference on the East Coast a number of years ago. After I settled into my hotel room, I opened the brochure detailing the week. It unfolded like a road map that fills the entire front seat of the car. There were dozens of seminars to choose from. *It will take forever to make a selection*, I thought. When my eyes caught the name of Ted Engstrom, I felt a surge of excitement. I had read half a dozen books by Ted and had deep respect and great admiration for his writings and his leadership of World Vision. *That settles it,* I thought. *I will attend Ted's seminar.* I was glad to get that decision behind me.

When the time came to hear what Ted had to say, I was filled with anticipation. I sat in the front row with pen in hand, ready to drink in his wisdom. He said he was going to begin with a short sermon that we would never forget. He suggested that in the very near future we take a piece of paper and make a list of all the things that we find ourselves doing that don't really make a significant difference: going shopping, mowing the lawn, changing the oil in the car, etc. He then advised us not to give our lives to the things on that list.

Now, he said, make a second list of the things that are truly and eternally important: spending time with people, growing, getting to know God, etc. He instructed us to give time and energy to the things on the second list. After this exercise, Ted proceeded into the topic at hand.

Decision and Discipline

When the conference was over, I was flying back to California at 30,000 feet. I reflected on the fact that I had heard many different speakers during the time, but I was overjoyed that I had gotten to listen to one of my heroes of the written page. The strange thing, though, was that I was still sorting out Ted's short, unforgettable sermon. Make two lists. Do the things on the one, but not on the other. All of a sudden it hit me—a blinding flash of the obvious.

Ted was saying two things. *Decide* what is truly important in life and what isn't. Then, *discipline* yourself to focus on what is important.

I don't think he was communicating that mowing the lawn, changing oil, or shopping is worthless. But as writer Leroy Eims used to say, "I don't want to be just one more guy pushing one more shopping cart through one more market." It's a matter of priorities and focus; I must be careful not to nickel-and-dime my time away while I miss the important things in my leadership role.

Stephen Covey reminds us, "The main thing is to keep the main thing the main thing." I should be concerned with being productive, not simply busy!

Many leaders don't do this on a consistent basis. They are

more reactive than proactive. They respond to what comes their way, rather than thinking things through ahead of time and choosing what is more important at any given moment. The squeaky wheel gets the oil. What makes the most noise and shouts the loudest often gets a leader's time and attention.

If it is true that 20 percent of our effort will produce 80 percent of our results (the famous Pareto Principle), we need to prayerfully and carefully figure out which 20 percent we will focus on. Jim Collins makes this observation:

> Most of us lead busy, but undisciplined lives. We have ever expanding "to do lists," trying to build momentum by doing, doing, doing—and doing more. And it rarely works. Those who built the good-to-great companies, however, made as much use of "stop doing" lists as the "to do lists." They displayed a remarkable discipline to unplug all sorts of extraneous junk. They displayed remarkable courage to channel their resources into only one or a few arenas.[1]

I often return to Jeremiah 42:3: "That the LORD your God may show us the way we should go, and the thing that we should do." I can't be everywhere, and I can't do everything. I need to make choices. That is what priorities are all about. Saying yes to one thing means saying no to something else. Saying yes to less is one of my goals. I say no to lots of things so that I can say yes to a few things.

Protecting My Purpose and Passion

As I cultivate my relationship with Jesus Christ and have clarity of and passion for my purpose, what will kill my effectiveness are unwise choices that are not commensurate with my purpose and passion. Proper priorities will protect my purpose and passion. Opportunities can pop up like the ducks at a shooting gallery. I can shoot them down, but I only have so many bullets and need to be careful what I aim for.

Priorities are like the banks of a river. They protect the river of a person's passion and purpose so that his or her energy is not dissipated all over the landscape. Clear priorities keep purpose and passion focused. It is a matter of constantly making choices about what you will do, where you will go, and what you will say yes to. These choices are the priorities—what is of value and importance. To stay emotionally and physically healthy you must make careful (and sometimes difficult) choices.

Management consultant and author Brian Tracy says, "Eighty percent of what you do on a daily basis needs to be intentional as opposed to responsive and should be directly tied to your purpose." For many (if not most) leaders, that is not the case. That's why there is so much frustration and so little productivity. The following story has motivated me to prioritize.

> [In the early 1900s,] Charles Schwab, then president of Bethlehem Steel, granted an interview to Ivy Lee, an extraordinary management consultant. Lee told Schwab that his consulting firm could uncover opportunities for improvement of the company's operations. Schwab said he already knew of more things that should be done than he and his staff could get to. What was needed was "not more knowing, but more going."
>
> "If you can show us a way to get more things done," Schwab said, "I'll be glad to listen to you. And, if it works, I'll pay you whatever you ask within reason."

Lee answered, "If that is what you want, I will show you a method that will increase your personal management efficiency, and that of anyone else who applies it, by at least fifty percent."

He handed Schwab a blank piece of paper and said, "Write down the most important things you have to do tomorrow." Schwab did as requested; it took about five minutes.

Lee then said, "Now, number them in the order of their true importance." This took a little longer because Schwab wanted to be sure of what he was doing.

Finally Lee instructed, "The first thing tomorrow morning, start working on item Number 1, and stay with it until it is completed. Then take item Number 2 the same way. Then Number 3, and so on. Don't worry if you don't complete everything on the schedule. At least you will have completed the most important projects before getting to the less important ones. . . .

"Do this every working day," Lee went on. "After you have convinced yourself of the value of this system, have your men try it. Try it as long as you like, and then send me your check for whatever you think the idea is worth."

In a few weeks, Charles Schwab sent Ivy Lee a check for $25,000 [the equivalent of $250,000 today].

Schwab reportedly stated that this lesson was the most profitable one he learned in his business career. It was later said that this was the plan largely responsible for turning a little steel company into one of the largest steel producers in the world. It also helped make Charles Schwab a multimillionaire.[2]

A Prioritized "Do" List

Oh, the beauty of a simple but powerful idea. I have told the Ivy Lee story countless times in seminars I conduct on time management. I then ask, "How many of you have heard of this idea—a 'do' list—before?" Almost everyone raises their hand. I ask them to note that it is a prioritized do list, which is different and more effective than a laundry list of things to do. Then I ask, "How many of you begin each day by creating such a list, prioritizing the items, and then planning your day accordingly?" I get a lot of embarrassed looks.

The idea is well known, widely accepted, but seldom used on a consistent basis. I personally begin every day by thoughtfully and prayerfully writing my prioritized list. If I don't create a daily plan that is a reflection of my God-given purpose and direction in life, there are sufficient numbers of people who will create a plan for me. I have those in my life who would say with smiles on their faces, "Dave, God loves you and I have a wonderful plan for your life."

An Intentional Process

But simply having a prioritized list is not enough. Last week, I was sitting with a leader at a fish-and-chips fast-food restaurant in Seattle. He had some SMART goals that he was sharing with me: goals that are Simple, Measurable, Attainable, Relevant, and Timely. As I began to ask him how this one or that one was going, I quickly realized that it wasn't. The problem was that he had it written down but had not scheduled it so that it could be carried out in a timely fashion. I grabbed a piece of paper and wrote out the following for us to discuss:

Goals   Plans   Priorities   Schedule   Execution   Evaluation

That same evening I had a young architect over for coaching. I showed him the same process, but quickly realized there were two pieces missing that should precede the first step—purpose and passion. So, adding to the list above, we now have:

1. Purpose—what I am called to accomplish in life
2. Passion—a sense of enthusiasm about my purpose and direction
3. Goals—where I want to go
4. Plans—what I am going to do to get there
5. Priorities—how I will arrange my plans to get there
6. Schedule—when I will actually do it
7. Execution—just do it
8. Evaluation—assessment of what happened, and how I can improve the process

A prioritized do list needs to be in context with the other seven elements. I realize that this is basic, and maybe even boringly elementary. But I am amazed at how many leaders I know and with whom I work that blow through their days of work and ministry feeling frustrated, unproductive, and unfruitful for the kingdom and don't know why. I think a big part of the frustration is found in their failure to follow the flow diagrammed above, from purpose through evaluation.

There is great advantage in being intentional in what you do, and in taking initiative to make life happen instead of merely letting life happen. It helps to have a clear idea of where you want to go and then select prioritized steps that will get you there. Taking time to prayerfully prioritize exponentially increases your chances of reaching a desired end.

A Clear Purpose Is the Driver

It must begin with a clear purpose. Purpose is the foundation for everything. It gives birth to passion that sings within you as you delve into daily leadership responsibilities. It is accompanied by a sense of joy in knowing that you are making a significant contribution. Out of your purpose and passion you set goals to help you get to where God wants you to be. To reach those goals you create action steps, a prioritized do list. You arrange them in the order of their true importance (remember Schwab and Lee), taking deadlines into consideration. Then you decide when you will do them, execute them as planned, and continually evaluate how you are progressing toward your desired goal.

This simple and intentional process will increase any leader's joy and fruitfulness. In many of us there is the temptation to try to do too much, to violate the principle of Sabbath, to be the savior of all mankind, and to travel at breakneck speeds. This brings us to the last of the five components of the leadership wheel: pacing.

CHAPTER 5:

The Leader's Pacing

"Don't rush me.
The hurrier I go the behinder I get."

SIGN AT A WORKSTATION

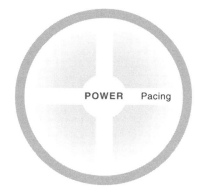

POWER Pacing

It didn't seem to make any difference what I ate—my stomach would bother me, regardless. I decided to take a Tums antacid after eating. It helped for a while, but within a few days, the discomfort returned. I upped the ante and began to take Tums before and after eating. Again, it helped at first, and then I was back to square one. It occurred to me that something might be seriously wrong. Maybe I had cancer of the stomach, bleeding ulcers, or some unthinkable terminal illness. This was particularly unnerving since I was only in my midtwenties at the time. Great health was not a trademark in the Kraft family, and the memory of that fact set my mind to worrying. I was in big trouble.

Finally, I bit the bullet and set up an appointment with the family doctor. He arranged for me to undergo an upper-GI examination. O happy day! After a few days, I came back to his office for the feared news. I was, of course, expecting the worst. He scooted his little three-legged stool over to me and looked me right in the eye and said, "Dave, there is nothing wrong with you. It's all stress related." Then he said something that I still think about to this day. "You're going to have to slow down!"

Slow down? Why would I want to do that?

I Learn the Hard Way

I was twenty-five, firmly committed to Christian ministry, working sixty hours a week for the Postal Department, and had something going on every night. I was Mr. Super Christian: young, full of ideas, and invincible. Slow down? Well, I guess I was going to have to, or else. I didn't even want to think about what "or else" might mean.

From that moment, I became a student of stress, balance, emotionally induced illnesses, pacing, and relaxation. Learning how to relax was a new concept to me. I was the burn-the-candle-at-both-ends-and-pray-fervently-for-more-wax kind of guy. Even today, I am by no means out of the woods. I am like an alcoholic who is one drink away from total disaster. I am a well-organized, goal-oriented, fast-paced, type A idiot. I know that my personality will never change.

But I can change the pace at which I travel and develop a healthy view of Sabbath that will prolong my purpose and passion. Actually, I don't mind being an organized, goal-oriented, fast-paced person. I am focused and intentional and get a lot done. But—and this is a big one—I need to be very careful not to overstep my God-given capacity and limits.

What Happened to Sabbath?

In a Sunday newspaper, I ran across the following:

> In the relentless busyness of modern life, we have lost the rhythm between action and rest. There is a universal refrain: I am so busy. As it all piles endlessly upon itself, the whole experience of being alive begins to melt into one enormous obliga-

tion. Sabbath time is a revolutionary challenge to the violence of overwork. Many of us, in our desperate drive to be successful and care for our many responsibilities, feel terrible guilt when we take time to rest.[1]

I believe that most leaders travel too fast and attempt to do too much. If priorities *protect* my purpose and passion, then pacing *prolongs* it. Someone said, "I am running on fumes and don't know where the next gas station is." That's the thought in Psalm 139:3: "You chart the path ahead of me and tell me where to stop and rest. Every moment, you know where I am" (TLB).

In my mind's eye, I see myself driving at top speed down the highway of life. On the left I see the sign that tells me a rest stop is just ahead. I have a choice: stop for a needed break, or put the pedal to the metal and press ahead. If I am listening, I will hear the Lord whisper in my ear to pull off the highway and take a break. This gives me the opportunity to recharge my emotional, physical, and spiritual batteries, and then to take up the journey with new strength.

I think that if the Lord were an officer of the law, he would give many of us a speeding ticket. Is there a speed limit for life and ministry? It's called the gauge of God-given capacity. We are not all the same.

A Lesson from the Rubber Band

We don't have the same gifts, personality, or capacity. I think people are like rubber bands, which come in all sizes and shapes. Some are small and some are large. A small rubber band can only be stretched so far. It has limits. A rubber band that is larger can obviously be stretched further. Regardless of how big or small the rubber band, it can only be stretched for so long, and then it needs to go back to a resting position. If it is stretched too far and stays there too long, it will snap.

We have all had the experience of picking up something that was wrapped with a rubber band for a long time, only to have it snap when we touched or moved it. Likewise, leaders need to determine what size their capacity is and how long they can remain in a stretched situation before they need a pause—whether emotional or physical.

Prolonged stretching with no rest will eventually bring about serious problems. Pacing is a matter of determining one's God-given capacity and deciding when to take breaks on the highway of life.

I Learned from a Race

In the early '80s I was living in the San Francisco Bay area. I had some friends who were into running races. I had jogged for a good many years but had never entered a race. I was invited to a race and lined up with Bob at the starting line. Bob gave me the best advice I've ever received for running in road races as well as life races. He told me not to try and keep up with the pack but to run my own pace and be true to what I was capable of. He warned me that the temptation would be to start out fast and try to stay up with the front-runners, which I could do for a few hundred feet.

"If you try to keep up," he warned, "you will never finish the seven-mile race, but will drop out after a mile." To this day,

I remember that advice. I had a great race and finished with energy as I ran at my individual pace.

It is so easy to try to be like other people, attempting to emulate their capacity, gifts, and personality. It takes a lot of grace to remain true to who God made you to be. Walt Disney put it well when he said, "The more you are like yourself, the less you are like anybody else, and that's what makes you unique."

A big-game hunter was traveling with a group of locals and was pushing them hard to cover a lot of ground each day. One day when he arose and was ready to start, they were just sitting there. In anger and frustration, he spoke to the interpreter to get them moving and demanded to know why they weren't responding. The answer was that "they were waiting for their souls to catch up with their bodies." Careful pacing does exactly the same thing. Sometimes our schedules and egos are writing checks our bodies can't cash. We are wise to allow for our souls to catch up, but how a leader does so can vary. Personally, I practice the following:

1. Take a full day off each week and limit my work hours.
2. Plan a full day alone for a spiritual retreat on a monthly basis.
3. Make sure I have some fun each week doing things that make me laugh.
4. Limit the number of evenings I am not at home.

Every once in a while, I am in contact with leaders who take no vacations or a weekly day off. They claim, "I just have too much to do." This is a clear violation of the biblical concept of Sabbath, the mandate to take adequate time off for rest and recreation.

Getting the leadership wheel rolling is basic to leadership fruitfulness and longevity. I take an hour prayer-run four days a week and allow my mind and spirit to review. I pray over each of the five pieces of the wheel, asking the Lord to make it clear to me how I'm doing.

Thinking Things Through

Part One

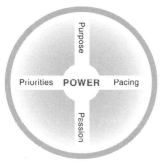

1. Review the five elements of the leadership wheel. How are you doing?
2. How is your walk with the Lord? Are you getting good quality time alone with him?
3. Do you have a purpose statement? If not, start writing one.
4. Do you sense passion in what you are doing, or are you feeling ho-hum?
5. Are you working from a prioritized do list? If not, why not start one right now?
6. Are you trying to do too much by attempting to keep everybody happy? Does that keep you moving at an insane pace?
7. As you look at each component of the leadership wheel, rate yourself on a scale of one to five (one being poor and five being excellent).
8. Pick one area to start with and create some action items for yourself that would help you invest in that area.

Formation

How do you know God has called you? Are you a person of strong inner character who can be trusted? Do you have the gifts that are essential to leadership? Are you a lifelong learner who consistently pursues growth opportunities? In this section, we will explore the following key areas of a leader's formation:

- Calling
- Gifts
- Character
- Growth

CHAPTER 6:

The Leader's Calling

"The need is not the call."

OSWALD CHAMBERS

This chapter is primarily for leaders in full-time vocational Christian ministry. If you're not in that category or don't see yourself there in the future, this will help you understand the challenges and pressures faced by those in such a role. You will learn how essential it is for these leaders to experience a call. You will also know how to pray for your pastor and others who are in full-time vocational Christian ministry.

Calling and Purpose

The concept of a call is not as prominent in Christian leadership circles as it was at one time. It's rather a slippery concept to get your head around. In yesteryear, leaders often talked about their call to the ministry or their call to a leadership role. When I connected with The Navigators for training, one of the first things we studied was the idea of being called. I was forced to ask myself questions such as, "Has God called me into vocational ministry with The Navigators?" and "How do I find out?"

Calling is a subjective but extremely important element in being a Christian leader. It's sort of like being in love. You can't exactly explain it, but you know when you've experienced it. There is a close correlation between purpose, discussed in Part One, and calling.

Finding your unique purpose is a result of reflecting on your experiences and interests. This reflection results in a statement of who you are and what you are about. Your purpose originates from within and is fine-tuned through a process of analysis and self-examination. A calling, on the other hand, comes from without.

Calling has to do with the God of the universe speaking into your life and circumstances, expressing his will. All Christians are enjoined to serve God by functioning in the body of Christ. At the same time, however, those who are serving in full-time positions of leadership in the church should experience the clear call of God on their life. There is too much at stake to simply fill a slot or assume a responsibility based solely on feeling, desire, or ambition.

Such leaders should work through the process of looking within at their interests, bents, and experiences. By doing this, they are able to determine their compelling purpose and, at the same time, expect a call from without. This call may be similar to the burning bush of Moses, or the Damascus road experience of Paul. Or it may be a quiet, slow process. In either case, a clear, deep, intuitive sense emerges that God has laid his hand on you for a specific and predetermined task. A call from God can come at any time in relationship to the clear awareness of one's purpose. In many cases, the call precedes the purpose. God called Moses first and then explained what he had in mind for him. Similarly, God first called Paul, and then gave him his assignment.

I would like to see the concept of calling revived so that it might receive some fresh and creative attention today. It could be the missing link in God-anointed ministry. I realize that all Christians are to serve and use their gifts. But, in another sense, there is the need for a fresh generation of visionary leaders who are called by God to *lead* the charge in a powerful new way.

It is this group of leaders that would do well to have the burning coal from the fire of God's altar placed on their lips and lives (Isa. 6:1–8). The need for such leaders to bring the touch of God on ministry is great. It is the opposite of simply fulfilling a leadership slot in ministry. The present dearth of inspirational, anointed, called, visionary leaders is incredible.

Everything I read, hear, and see confirms this fact. Where is the next generation of God-called, God-anointed leaders?

My Call

I worked for the U.S. Post Office in the early 1960s. I was very happy there, and I could have stayed there until retirement. As I began to grow in my relationship with the Lord, a certain stirring took place. It was not something I planned, prayed for, or sought after. It just happened.

I had a sense that God had something else in mind for me. No one had talked to me or suggested I consider another career or vocation. God broke into my nice cozy world and started something. There was no doubt in my mind that I would not be working at the post office for the rest of my life. I can't entirely explain why.

I was restless, expectant, excited, yet clueless. But I knew that somewhere, somehow, and at some time God had something for me that was far different from what I was currently doing.

Others who knew me came to the same conclusion. I had no idea then how different it would be.

A group was forming at my church for those who felt God was calling them into full-time Christian work. I showed up. As we went around, each shared plans about the Bible school or Christian organization they had in mind. When my turn came, I simply shared that I had a conviction that God was calling me to some type of ministry but that I had no idea what. In due time, however, the plan unfolded.

The power of that call helped me immensely when I hit the tough places during my thirty-eight years of service with The Navigators, eight of which were spent as a missionary in Sweden. When I doubted, wanted to give up, or experienced criticism or misunderstanding, the clarity of my call helped me to press ahead. My call was and remains today a deep stake in my life, a watershed point in my journey.

The Four Spiritual Calls

Let's put this mysterious but important call in perspective. There are four calls that I can identify:

1. The call to salvation
2. The call to discipleship
3. The call to service
4. The call to leadership

Salvation

The first call is the call to salvation. Depending on your theological position, a call is issued to the elect or to any who will respond. "Come to me, all who labor and are heavy laden" (Matt. 11:28); "Whoever believes in him should not perish" (John 3:16); "Believe in the Lord Jesus, and you will be saved" (Acts 16:31). The type of leader I refer to in this book is one who has clearly responded to the call to salvation.

Discipleship

The second call is a call to discipleship. This means that one is a fully devoted and committed follower of Jesus Christ. Luke 14 goes into great detail on this call. This should be part and parcel of the call to salvation and should occur at the same time. There is an ongoing, raging debate: Can one truly be a Christian without being a fully devoted disciple of Jesus? I would seriously question a call to Christian leadership for one who has not clearly submitted his life to Jesus as Lord.

I agree with the premise that if he is not Lord of all, he is not Lord at all. Leadership is not about popularity or personality or charm. It is about fulfilling God's purpose in life. One reason so many church leaders fail is that their motivation for stepping into a responsibility does not have its source in God, but in self.

Service

The call to service is next. First, am I more than a Christian who drops a few dollars in the plate and attends church when it fits my schedule? I must be one who is sold out for the cause of Jesus Christ. Then I am ready to serve. Service is the rent we pay for our space in life, motivated by the love of Jesus!

I believe in the little big principle from Luke 16:10: "One who is faithful in a very little is also faithful in much." I am a true believer and follower of Jesus. I am serving, and with his help I desire to make a difference. Out of this context comes the next step for certain Christ-followers: a call to significant, and in some cases, full-time vocational ministry. The goal is to develop servants of Jesus Christ, and from these servants he calls leaders.

Leadership

A call to full-time leadership is what we are primarily dealing with in this chapter. I am talking about a clear, unmistakable sense of God's hand on you for some distinct leadership contribution or role—perhaps yet undefined.

This call is vital for leaders who last. Experiencing a specific, personal call from God helps you to persevere. However, if you are in a leadership role for the sake of your own glory and reputation, for accolades and affirmation from others, or to feel needed, you can easily lose heart when affirmation is missing. If you are doing what you do because God has clearly called you, it strengthens your ability to hang in there. Paul refers to this in 2 Corinthians 4:1: "Therefore, having this ministry by the mercy of God, we do not lose heart."

Both Isaiah and Jeremiah detail their clear callings from God in the early chapters of their books. It was this calling that enabled them to stick it out in the tough times. I sometimes wonder: is the reason many do not last because they entered the ministry without a clear call from God? A clear and compelling call is essential.

In the past, it was assumed that, if you were in a position of leadership, God had spoken to and called you. You were expected to tell your story. Bible schools, seminaries, faith-based organizations, and missionary movements would, as a matter of course, ask about your call to ministry. It was dealt with in the application you submitted.

Charles "Prince of Preachers" Spurgeon conducted interviews to ascertain the calling of potential students of Spurgeon College. If their calling was not clear, they were not admitted. Today, however, it seems there is hardly a whisper about being called.

As far as I know, there is no simple recipe for discerning one's call. It's not a matter of steps one, two, and three. It is a result of wrestling with God, examining one's motivation, and sensing the touch of God, the unmistakable voice of God speaking to your soul. It is also helpful to consult with those who know you well.

Oswald Chambers has this to say in *My Utmost for His Highest*:

> There comes the baffling call of God in our lives also. The call of God can never be stated explicitly, it is implicit. The call of God is like the call of the sea; no one hears it but the one who has the nature of the sea in him.
>
> It cannot be stated definitely what the call of God is to because His call is to be in comradeship with himself for His own purpose, and the test is to believe that God knows what He is after.[1]

With a clear word from God, you will have an overwhelming conviction that you can do no other than what he is calling you to do. There is a "fire in the belly," a pull, a strange attraction to some aspect of leadership that cannot be humanly explained. It comes from on high, not from within; from God and not from men. You can't get away from it. Often, other people spot it before you do.

Evaluate Your Calling

You need people who will help by asking questions like:

- What do you enjoy doing?
- What do you avoid doing? Why?
- For what do you wish to be remembered?
- How might the offer of money or a promotion sidetrack you from your true calling?
- What would your life look like if it turned out well?

There are many people who have entered full-time leadership positions who are not called, will not last, and will soon quit—or worse yet, they will stay on until retirement. Professor Eddie Gibbs of Fuller Seminary put it well when he said, "The presence in seminaries of those who ought not to be there is due to their having fulfilled the academic entry requirements but without any assessment of their sense of call to ministry, their suitability or their individual gifting." [2]

For many, it's just a job—with no fire burning within! This was affirmed in a recent article I read, which stated the following: "One-thousand four-hundred pastors leave the ministry each month because of stress, disillusionment, or forced termination. In the Southern Baptist Convention, 98 pastors are terminated monthly."[3]

Why is this happening? I don't want to be overly simplistic, but I wonder how much is due to leaders who enter the ministry without a distinct call from God. There are also those who are clearly called but are afraid to respond or feel inadequate—as did most leaders in the Old Testament, who were called by God for some task way over their heads.

Are you a more experienced leader? Allow me to challenge you to watch for younger, future leaders to whom God is speaking and calling. Take the initiative to encourage them to step up to the plate. Are you thinking about a full-time leadership responsibility? If you can see yourself doing anything else, then do that! But if you are convinced deep in your heart that God has called you to lead, then lead as you trust God in the midst of your fears. I have been out of my comfort zone and over my head for most of my life as a leader, and it has helped me to develop trust, not depend on myself, and experience Jesus in ways I would not have by staying comfortable.

Now, on to the crucial area of gifting.

CHAPTER 7

The Leader's Gifts

"Everyone has some gifts, therefore all should be encouraged. Nobody has all the gifts, therefore all should be humble. All gifts are from the Lord, therefore all should be contented."

ARTHUR T. PIERSON

I heard about a bricklayer whose brother was a famous violinist. The bricklayer was talking with the head of the construction company where he worked. "It must be great to have a brother who is known around the world," said the executive. Then he added, "Of course, we must accept the fact that talent isn't equally distributed—even in the same family."

"That's right," replied the bricklayer. "Why, my brother doesn't know the first thing about bricklaying. It's a good thing he can afford to pay others to build a house for him."

We are all gifted differently. One person is not better or worse than another in the body of Christ because of his or her gifting. The Lord has placed each of us in the family to fulfill certain functions. How I am gifted is God's choice, not mine. The leader who lasts needs to be gifted in certain ways in order to make the maximum contribution.

Our purpose in this chapter is to consider those gifts that are essential to carry out the role of leadership.

Gifts Necessary for Leadership

A lot has been written on the subject of spiritual gifts. There is no question that the Bible teaches about gifts; however, there are two common issues worth mentioning. The first is the question of whether the lists we have in Romans 12, 1 Corinthians 12, Ephesians 4, and 1 Peter 4 are complete lists of gifts or simply a sampling of some of the gifts. A second issue concerns what part gifts play in determining one's role in the body of Christ.

It is not my desire to further the debate. However, I do believe the leaders we are referring to in this book need certain kinds of gifts that enable them to carry out their leadership functions and responsibilities.

If you poll people about what sort of things a spiritual leader does, you will get varied responses. The new kind of leaders I am discussing are ones who will reach the finish line. They should carry out at least four functions contained in my working definition of a leader: they should shepherd, develop, equip, and empower those being led. It takes a certain kind of person to perform the above-mentioned functions. Everyone is not designed to be a leader any more than everyone is not designed to be a teacher or an administrator.

Speaking Gifts versus Serving Gifts

I have come to the conclusion that all of the gifts listed in the above passages fit into *speaking* abilities or *serving* abilities. First Peter 4:11 says, "Whoever speaks, as one who speaks oracles of God; whoever serves, as one who serves by the strength that God supplies—in order that in everything God may be glorified through Jesus Christ. To him belong glory and dominion forever and ever. Amen." In this verse, speaking and serving are both mentioned.

After many years of teaching on the subject of spiritual gifts and working with hundreds of people to help them determine their gifting, it seems the gifts of a leader tend more toward speaking than serving. Bobby Clinton of Fuller Seminary refers to these gifts as *word gifts*. A true leader is gifted and skilled at using words to shephord, develop, equip, and empower followers and potential leaders.

The leader who lasts needs to have word gifts. This is not to say that they don't serve. But what distinguishes them as leaders is their ability to use words to accomplish the mission, communicate an agreed upon vision, climb the mountain, and reach the goal. George Barna, author of numerous books and an expert on church health and growth, has said more than once that only 6 percent of senior pastors believe they have the gift of leadership.

I am going out on a limb with this next statement: if a person's gift mix is not predominantly in the speaking category, that person should not consider a major leadership roll. They would fit better in a support role. I am not saying that a leader doesn't serve or that serving roles are inferior to speaking roles. But I am saying that leaders serve best by leading through word gifts to move people along from point A to point B. They encourage, exhort, develop, equip, and inspire through language or words.

Leaders need to be full of faith, energy, and God-given dreams that carry others along in their wake. Everywhere you look in the Old and New Testaments, you find that the Lord tapped individuals who were wired together this way. Nehemiah, David, Paul, and Peter are a few that spring to mind. They were leaders who spent a lot of time communicating and using words!

People in leadership roles who don't possess speaking gifts get tired, worn out, and discouraged quickly. Many are in leadership rolls that they are not gifted to fulfill. They struggle greatly and bear little fruit, and they often quit or are removed. It is difficult to perform a role for which one is not fitted and equipped. You don't have to have a super personality or be extremely outgoing or charismatic. You can be very extroverted and not have these essential leadership gifts, and you can be introverted and possess them in abundance. There are many leaders who are on the quiet side. But these leaders nonetheless have word gifts.

A leader I once served under was a good teacher, but he was not able to energize or motivate those of us under his leadership to believe great things or attempt great things for God. I began to have a sense that he was not in the right place, and I soon discovered that others felt the same way.

One day, several of us prayerfully and carefully approached him with our observations. He was incensed that we had the nerve to question his leadership ability. However, shortly after that confrontation, he accepted a teaching role in another city and became much happier. He now had a good fit. We were better off with a new leader who had the necessary gifts, and he was better off with a job that really suited the way God had designed him.

The Right Place for the Right Reasons

If, as George Barna has noted, 94 percent of senior pastors are correct in their belief that they don't have the gift of leadership, is it any wonder that, according to church consultant Bill Easum, 85 percent of the churches in the United States have either plateaued or are dying? When are we going to wake up and deal with ego and insecurity and humbly take roles that God intended for us, rather than those we desire for the wrong reasons?

If you are in leadership and feel frustrated, or if you are thinking about taking on a leadership role, I urge you to take an honest look at your gifting, experience, and passion. Listen clearly to what others are saying. Ascertain whether you have a leadership role to play and have the God-given abilities to carry it out. There's too much at stake to take leadership lightly and step into it for glory, applause, power, attention, or monetary rewards.

There are three things that can point the way to whether you are suited for a leadership role:

1. Your gifts, discovered through gift inventories
2. Your experience and passions, analyzed through trends and tendencies in your personal history that answer this question: what has the Lord blessed in the past?
3. Your feedback from others who know you and have observed you

One Size Doesn't Fit All

I had the privilege of working for many years in the same organization with Lorne Sanny, who was president of The Navigators for thirty years. He referred to himself as "the reluctant leader." He is not the stereotypical leader: six feet tall with an impressive or electric personality. Instead, he is a quiet sort of man with a gentle spirit. You would never have picked him out of a room full of people as the leader of a large, multinational Christian organization.

But in his quiet and gentle way, Lorne was called and gifted to lead The Navigators through all those years. He was not like Saul, who stood head and shoulders above his countrymen. He was more like David, a man after God's own heart.

Lorne didn't seek leadership or strive for it. It came to him because others saw certain gifts in him. He spoke quietly, but when he finished speaking, you felt energized and wanted to go out and make a difference with your life. I certainly did!

Thus, we are not talking about certain personality profiles. Leaders that last come in all shapes, sizes, and personality types. We are not talking about physical stature or appearance. We are simply talking about a man or a woman whom God has called and given certain kinds of abilities that enable them to shepherd, develop, equip, and empower others to be part of reaching God-pleasing objectives.

Next, the heart of the matter: Christlike character!

CHAPTER 8

The Leader's Character

"The greatest crisis in the world today is a crisis of leadership, and the greatest crisis in leadership is a crisis of character."

HOWARD HENDRICKS

A man visited a carnival with his daughter. She asked her dad if she could have cotton candy. When the vendor handed it to her, he said, "Are you sure you can eat all of that by yourself, young lady?"

The little girl replied, "Sure, 'cause I'm bigger on the inside than I am on the outside."

That is what character is all about: how big you are on the inside. Character can be defined as "who and what you are when no one is looking."

A few years back, a huge billboard alongside a well-traveled road where I lived said, "Character Counts." These words stared you in the face as you drove by. Character does count. It counts a lot. However, things that have been happening in the political and business world would suggest that it doesn't count and, furthermore, that people can rise to acceptable levels of achievement and then sustain themselves without character.

Character versus Competence

In many quarters there seems to be a tendency to overlook a lack of character in one's personal and private life in exchange for a high degree of success in one's professional life. Author Bill Thrall says, "The dysfunctions of many leaders are rooted in a common reality: Their capacities have been extensively trained while their character has been merely presumed." Thrall also reminds us that the ladder of success is actually composed of two ladders: capacity (which can also be referred to as "competency") and character. Both must be climbed at the same time. With each step I take on the capacity (competency) ladder, I need to also step on the character ladder. The two ladders need to be integrated.[1]

Capacity and *competence* are like gliders. They can fly, but not indefinitely, and they might not hold up during turbulent times. Who you are will take you much further than what you can do. *Character* will stand the test of time and hold up when the wind howls and the storm rages around you.

Most leaders focus too much on competence and too little on character. More people plateau, quit, or are relieved of their leadership responsibility over character issues than competency issues. In fact, General Schwarzkopf (of Gulf War fame) said, "Ninety-nine percent of leadership failures are failures of character."[2] Bill Clinton and Richard Nixon are both cases in point.

The primary passages on leadership qualifications in the Bible (1 Timothy 3 and Titus 1) talk mainly of character, not competence. A reading of these two passages reveals that only one competency trait is listed: "teaching." Everything else refers to character lived out in the context of relationships.

The most important of these relationships is the leader's family. This is the testing and proving grounds and the reason why 1 Timothy 3 and Titus 1 put such a huge emphasis on the leader's family. This subject has been the centerpiece of many books on leadership, and rightly so!

What People Value in Leaders

In their landmark book, *The Leadership Challenge*, authors James Kouzes and Barry Posner surveyed nearly 1,500 managers from around the country in a study sponsored by the American Management Association. They asked the following open-ended question: "What values (personal traits or characteristics) do you look for and admire in your superiors?" More than 225 different values, traits, and characteristics were identified. Subsequent content analysis by several independent judges reduced these items into fifteen categories. The category that got the most frequent response was *integrity*. They defined integrity as being truthful and trustworthy, and having convictions.[3]

In my thirty-eight years on The Navigators staff, it became increasingly clear to the leadership that we focused too much on competence and not enough on character development. The organization is now making some significant changes by investing time and money in improving the way we develop the character of our leaders.

One of my all-time favorite coaches is John Wooden of the UCLA Bruins. He achieved the unbelievable by winning ten NCAA basketball championships in twelve years—seven in a row. John is the only man ever elected to the College Basketball Hall of Fame as both player and coach. He was, and still is, a sterling example of Christian character in action.

In his wonderful book, *They Call Me Coach*, John Wooden tells us his story firsthand. Published in 1972, the book captures the essence of this man. It is full of the wisdom of an athlete who put his faith and character into practice on the court, both as a player and as a coach. The book has great quotes on character issues; let me give you the one I liked best: "Be more concerned with your character than with your reputation, because your character is what you really are while your reputation is merely what others think you are."[4]

I'll be the first to admit that I have paid entirely too much attention to what others think about my reputation and not enough to what I am in the core of my character.

I conduct a seminar entitled, "Critical Factors for Success." In it, I make the point that the key elements that lead to success are contained in three categories:

1. Character in your person
2. Caring in your relationships
3. Competence in your endeavors

By far, the most important is character. Having Christlike character as the bedrock of my life is absolutely essential and foundational to everything else.

With God's help as I develop my Christian character, significant change will take place in my relationships and my competency. In carrying out leadership tasks in the context of teamwork, the key is building relationships of trust. Arthur Friedman tells us, "Men of genius are admired. Men of wealth are envied. Men of power are feared, but only men of character are trusted." Now that is something to chew on. Can we really accomplish anything of value without the trust-filled collaboration of others? And can there ever be trust without solid character?

Valuable Lessons from Fortune 500 Companies

Senior executives at companies such as Enron, ImClone, Tyco, Arthur Andersen, and WorldCom were riding high on their image and performance before their true character was revealed and spoiled the party. The excesses of these executives helped destroy corporations, hundreds of thousands of good jobs, and the retirement security of millions. (I am sure that before this book is published there will be many more to add to this sad and sorry list.)

It is tempting to come to the conclusion that men and women of character are an endangered species in politics and business. What is even more frightening is that lack of character is increasingly showing up in Christian leadership. Pastors and other leaders are often forced to resign due to moral failure.

But it is encouraging to read examples of sterling character. Quite frankly, I'm tired of reading studies that tell us there is no marked difference between those who profess Christ and those who don't. There needs to be a difference. There *has* to be a difference.

The Lear Jet Story

Bill Lear, inventor, aviator, and business leader, held more than 150 patents. In 1963, the first Lear Jet made its debut, and the next year production on the Lear Jet began. But it was not all roses. Early on, two of his Lears crashed mysteriously. He immediately grounded the fifty-five he had sold so that he could determine the cause.

This is quite a contrast to some car manufacturers who leave certain models on the road even though they know they have production flaws. They count on clever lawyers to rescue them, rather than honestly dealing with their mistakes and doing a total recall.

Money is clearly more important to these companies than lives. Not so with Bill Lear. Grounding the fifty-five planes was costly. In addition, doubts were raised in the minds of potential buyers.

But Bill Lear went one step further. He discovered he couldn't determine what caused the fatal crashes without simulating the conditions under which they occurred. So he flew one of his own jets, almost succumbing to the same fate as the other two pilots. He managed to get through the tests and verify the defects, and he replaced the defective part in all fifty-five planes. Because of the loss, it took him two years to rebuild the business. But he never regretted his decision. What a leader! He lost money and risked his own life, but he never compromised his character.[5]

My Own Character Development Journey

For many years, it has been the habit of my life to ask God to show me some area of my character that needs attention. I usually give thought to this at the end of a year. One year, it was painfully clear to me that I needed to be more generous with my time and money.

I began in earnest in January of that year, praying, getting others to pray, and thinking a good deal about what being more generous would look like for me. I decided not to mention this to my wife and four children, hoping they would see a difference.

In November of that particular year, I decided to share this work in progress with my youngest daughter, Karina, as I drove her to school one day. I told her I had been praying and working all year on generosity, and then announced to her the character trait for next year.

She quickly stopped me and told me that I needed to work on generosity for one more year. We agreed that I had made good progress but that I had a long way to go. We laughed and realized that I would be working on generosity and all other character qualities until the day I die. Character development is not a short-term project, but a lifelong pursuit.

King David

In a study I did on leadership comparing the lives of David and Saul, the issue of character in relation to a leader was quite revealing. David is often regarded as a leadership success and Saul a leadership failure. Buried in one of the psalms is one of David's secrets: "With upright heart he shepherded them and guided them with his skillful hand" (Ps. 78:72). Here we see the combination of competence and character. David led his people with a heart of integrity (character) and skillful hands (competence). These qualities should always go hand in hand in the life of a leader.

King David was by no means perfect, but deep inside he was a man of character. After his disastrous encounter with Bathsheba, he confessed his sin before God, as Psalms 32 and 51 attest. Saul, on the other hand, never rebounded from his sin and [e eventually died by deliberately falling on his own

you read through the Bible, you will see leaders rise

and fall over character issues. The books of Kings and Chronicles bear this out—they display the character failures of one leader after the other, with occasional exceptions.

Examples of Character Traits to Develop

With God's help, I am determined to prefer character to making money. This means I will prefer doing what's right to doing what's profitable. That's what character is all about: doing what's right, even if it hurts.

Here is a list of some essential character traits:

Gentleness	Transparency	Forgiveness
Tactfulness	Patience	Dependability
Thankfulness	Vulnerability	Honesty
Trust	Compassion	Encouragement
Humility	Affirmation	Self-control

1. Rank how you are doing on each descriptive quality. Use a scale from one to five (one being poor, five being excellent).
2. Pick one or two areas where you know God wants to do something in your life.
3. Write down what you can and will do to experience growth in that area.
4. Choose a person to whom you will make yourself accountable.

(Regarding item number 4: character is developed and exhibited in the context of relationships. It is hard to develop character in isolation. Even Robinson Crusoe had Friday. And in the film *Castaway*, Tom Hanks had Wilson.)

What we desperately need today are leaders who are called and gifted by God. We need leaders who are filled with the Spirit of God and marked by the kinds of character qualities listed in Galatians 5:22–23: "Love, joy, peace, patience, kindness, goodness, faithfulness, gentleness, self-control."

For me, the most important thing in life is to be a person of character. This means I am the same person at home as I am in public, and I am a leader who can be believed and trusted by my family and the people in my ministry. Character counts! It matters to God and it matters in leadership.

Another area that counts is continual growth, and we'll address that in the next chapter.

CHAPTER 9

The Leader's Growth

"It's what you learn after you know it all that counts."

JOHN WOODEN

Author Tom Peters observed, "If you're not scared, you're not growing."[1] Peters regularly puts himself in harm's way a dozen times a year or else he goes hopelessly stale. One of the worst mistakes you can make as a leader is putting your life on cruise control. Good, effective, and relevant leadership is all about lifelong learning. It is about being teachable, accountable, and proactive, and trying new things. Growth means taking calculated risks.

Finishing Well

What will it take to finish well? What will it take to get to the end of your road and realize that you are where you want to be, you are who you want to be, and you have done what God wants you to do? This is the question that is at the heart of this book. Bobby Clinton, whom I mentioned earlier, concluded that those he studied in the Bible, as well as other leaders he has observed, shared five characteristics that enabled them to finish well.

1. They maintained a vibrant, personal relationship with God right up to the end.

2. They maintained a learning posture and learned from various sources.
3. They lived by identifiable goals and were characterized by a good degree of self-control in their mind, will, and emotions.
4. They saw the need for meaningful, supportive personal relationships. They devoted time to developing a network of such intentional relationships, starting with their marriage and family.
5. They had a clear vision, strong biblical convictions, a great sense of perspective, and a lifelong commitment to pleasing and honoring the Lord through a daily, deliberate surrender to the lordship of Christ in all things.[2]

The second characteristic on Clinton's list is our focus in this chapter. Being an effective leader is a matter of being a lifelong learner, learning at all times, under all circumstances, from all sorts of people—even your kids!

"Dad, You Need to Work on This"

A few years ago, I was in the kitchen fixing something and carrying on a conversation with my daughter Sara. Suddenly, she looked up at me and said, "Dad, did you know that you have a problem with interrupting people? You need to do something about that." Her direct words were hard to listen to and receive, but I knew she was right. I began to seek God's help and grace in this area of my life. For me, the hardest people to learn from are those in my own family. I am often reminded of Ecclesiastes 4:13: "Better was a poor and wise youth than an old and foolish king who no longer knew how to take advice."

Things are changing so fast these days, and the frenetic

pace is constantly upping the demand on us. We need to stay up to date and relevant in our leadership in order to know what is going on with the people we lead. We need to be constantly learning, growing, stretching, getting out of our comfort zones, reading new things, and trying new things. Ongoing, lifelong learning is essential to the leadership process. What will carry you and me through to a good finish is our desire and determination to keep growing.

After a series of speaking engagements, author and church consultant Tom Bandy noted, "Amid all the cities I have visited this year, and out of all the church leaders I have coached, it amazes me how many leaders have simply stopped growing, or yearn to stop growing."[3]

Successful people in all walks of life, whether they are artists, inventors, scientists, or executives, never lose the spirit of a learner. They are like trees: when the tree stops growing, the fruit starts to rot.

How Fast Do You Learn?

During a flight, I read an interview with Jim Crupi of Strategic Leadership Solutions. He was asked, "What does the average business person need to know about the future?"

His response was, "Leaders are fundamentally going to have to change the way they lead and manage people. The speed of change is only going to get faster. Their experience is not as valuable as it used to be—only their ability to adjust, adapt."[4]

And then he made the statement that really caught my attention: "It's not what you've been taught that matters. It's how fast you can learn."

In baseball lingo, yesterday's home runs don't win today's ball games. What worked last year might not fit at all. What gave me results three years ago might be totally irrelevant to today's issues and opportunities. My ability to finish well, to stay relevant, and to remain vibrant and fresh in my leadership and in my walk with God is related to continued learning and growth. Leaders are learners. Learning is inherent in the word *discipleship*, which can be defined as "a student who follows another." Learning is the key to leadership survival in a changing culture that is traveling at warp speed.

Practical Suggestions for Growing Leaders

Learning is also essential to remaining spiritually alive and fresh in Jesus Christ. When you're through learning, you're through. Here are a handful of practical suggestions to help you in your learning to move from "what?"—information gathering—to "so what?"—so what am I going to do with the information?

Ask Questions

I am trying to ask more questions. It serves me well to recapture the heart of a child who will ask: Why is water wet? Why do big people stop growing? Who does God's job when he's on vacation?

God has given us one mouth but two ears, so we should be listening twice as much as we talk. Here are some questions I ask of others and myself:

- What am I hearing that is new or different from what I have previously believed or thought?

- Can you share with me how you arrived at your conclusion?
- What prejudices might I be holding that are making it hard for me to listen to this individual?
- What personal application is there in what I am hearing or seeing?

Catherine is responsible for the women's ministry at a megachurch. She is extremely gifted and articulate. She shared with me that the most important thing she was learning was being a better listener and asking lots of questions, rather than doing most of the talking. I am learning that as well, and in fact, it is at the top of my prayer list.

As a teacher and communicator, listening well does not come naturally for me. I read that the first rule of being a great student is asking good questions, and the first rule of being a growing disciple is to be a great student. Sometimes I find that the best thing I can do for someone is not giving the right answer, but asking the right question.

Read

I read all the time. I always have a book with me in the car, on the plane, in my briefcase, and in several rooms throughout my home. I try not to visit a doctor or dentist's office without taking something along to read that stimulates my thinking and expands my mental horizons. I subscribe to magazines and blogs that are full of creative ideas and paradigm-shifting thoughts. I am eager to keep learning, growing, and changing.

Formation

Write

Writing down what I am learning accentuates my capacity to grow. Dawson Trotman, founder of The Navigators, said, "Thoughts disentangle themselves passing over the lips and through the pencil tips." A review of previous notes and journaling from times with the Lord can establish benchmarks of my growth. I am constantly writing down ideas I glean from my Bible, other books, movies, music, magazine articles, signs in offices, conversations, conferences, and meetings. A few days ago I was listening to a song on a CD that stimulated my thinking, so I pulled over and wrote down some ideas for deeper reflection.

Things I write down are the foundations that later can nourish, challenge, and encourage others and myself. Some people collect coins or stamps. I collect ideas. I keep thoughts and ideas on my computer for quick access and have dozens of file folders with ideas I have harvested from my reading. Writing keeps me spiritually alive and alert so that I can faithfully respond to the Lord and his Word and stay relevant to my culture.

I once had lunch with a pastor friend of mine. During our time together, he visited the men's room. When he returned, he quickly grabbed a piece of paper and began writing hurriedly. When I asked him what he was writing, he told me it was something that he had seen on the bathroom wall: "Work as if you don't need the money. Love as if you have never been hurt. Dance as if no one is watching." I have been chewing on that one for a couple of weeks now. You never know where you're going to find a great thought that can trigger new vistas of understanding and personal growth.

Seriously Consider Radically Different Ideas

It's too easy for me to travel along the same rut in my learning patterns. I am determined to take time to examine and understand other points of view, even if they are radically different from or contradictory to my own. Philippians 2:4 says, "Let each of you look not only to his own interests, but also to the interests of others," which commentator John Phillips rendered, "learning to see things from other people's point of view" (PHILLIPS).

I am involved in a church with a majority of younger men and women, and I have many opportunities to practice this principle. Most of what I hear in talking with them is new, different, or downright confusing. But at age seventy, I am still an eager student.

I am stretched through listening, thinking, and asking frequent questions. At this stage, I have more questions than answers. Proverbs 24:32 comes in handy: "Then I saw and considered it; I looked and received instruction."

It has been my experience that one of the indicators that I am learning is that I am continuing to change as I allow God access to my innermost person. I want to invite those closest to me to both challenge and affirm me in the character issues of my life. Is there more evidence of the fruit of the spirit (love, joy, peace, patience, kindness, goodness, faithfulness, gentleness, and self-control) in my life? Is there less evidence of the works of the flesh (sexual immorality, impurity, sensuality, enmity, strife, jealousy, fits of anger, rivalries, dissensions, divisions; see Gal. 5:19–20)? If I am learning and growing, the answer to both questions will be yes—not because I am trying harder, but because I am listening to the Lord as I respond in obedience and allow him to change me from the inside out.

Being highly receptive to new ideas is a skill that can be learned. As I continue to grow and change, I am motivated to learn from any and all kinds of people. I want to acquire the habit of reaching out and constantly searching. I want my mind and spirit to be fertile ground into which worthwhile seeds can fall and grow.

Growing or Plateaued?

Howard Hendricks shares the story of a professor he had at Dallas Seminary who was in his study early in the mornings and late in the evenings. Howard walked by his home and saw him through the study window. One day curiosity got the better of him and he asked the old professor what motivated him to keep studying, assuming that by now he would have encountered almost everything and would be coasting into retirement. The wise old professor answered, "I would rather have my students drink from a flowing stream than a stagnant pool."[5]

This hits me hard and gives me a strong desire to continually be a living, life-giving stream, not a stagnant pool. It reminds me of the difference between the Sea of Galilee, through which the Jordan River flows, and the Dead Sea, which has no outlet. One is alive, the other dead.

A man applied for a new job. On the questionnaire, he was asked how many years of experience he had. He wrote sixteen. During the oral interview, this question was put to him, "Do you really have sixteen years of experience, or one year repeated fifteen times?"

I've been a follower of Jesus Christ for fifty years, and I could ask myself the same question: Do I have fifty years of learning and growing in Jesus, or one year repeated forty-nine times? Am I moving forward or treading water? Am I different today than I was last year? What specifically has changed? What am I doing differently? What have I stopped doing, and what have I started doing with God's grace? What habits have I developed or broken?

A lifelong learner asks all kinds of questions, reads broadly, writes down new ideas, learns from opposing thoughts, and is growing in Christian character. As I continue to learn, there is a freshness and excitement that is contagious. People who know me well experience me as a passionate and energetic person.

One of the main contributors to my growth is my commitment and determination to dip my bucket deeply and regularly into the well of new and fresh thinking. I trust that this chapter has motivated you to keep on learning. A lot is at stake. It is nothing less than your own effectiveness and the personal growth and progress of those you lead.

Thinking Things Through

Part Two

1. If you are in full-time vocational ministry, how would you explain your calling to somebody?
2. Take inventory of your gifts. Do you have word gifts? Does your gifting match your current ministry assignment? Do family and close friends concur?
3. Is there some aspect of your character that God has been speaking to you about? What steps can you take to grow in that area? To whom will you be accountable?
4. What are you doing to ensure you are a lifelong learner?

Fruitfulness

All that has been said up to this point has set the stage for moving toward your vision of the future and enlisting others to join you. If no one is following, you are taking a walk by yourself. Among those you lead and influence are future leaders. These leaders can be your lasting legacy! In this section, we explore the three primary avenues where leaders can impact others.

- Vision
- Influence
- Legacy

CHAPTER 10:

The Leader's Vision

"Leadership is the capacity to translate vision into reality."

WARREN B. BENNIS

In his classic work, *Servant Leadership*, Robert K. Greenleaf says,

> Not much happens without a dream. And for something great
> to happen, there must be a great dream. Behind every great
> achievement is a dreamer of great dreams. Much more than a
> dreamer is required to bring it to reality; but the dream must
> be there first.[1]

In Parts One and Two, I dealt with the kind of person the leader is: how he leads and develops himself. In Part Three, I will delve into how the leader impacts others. This person-to-person influence is at the heart of leadership. To lead means that you are a certain kind of person who travels in a specific direction and recruits other people to join you on your journey.

- *A Certain Kind of Person.* In Part One, I addressed the issue of how Christian leaders operate from a power base centered in the Lord Jesus Christ. They have a clear life purpose, which generates a sense of passion and excitement. They are careful to choose activities that are prioritized to help them accomplish that purpose. And they travel at a sane pace, to live as long as God intended. In Part Two, I said that these leaders have a sense of calling and a set of gifts that enable them to lead. These leaders are also growing in character, and they are lifelong learners.

- *A Specific Direction.* This deals with having a vision, which is covered in this chapter.
- *Recruiting Others.* These are the people who are on the journey with the leader and whom the leader is influencing by shepherding, developing, equipping, and empowering. This topic will be covered in chapters 11 and 12.

The simplest way I know how to think of leadership is in the above three areas. It is born out of our initial definition: "A Christian leader is a humble, God-dependent, team-playing servant of God who is called by God to shepherd, develop, equip, and empower a specific group of believers to accomplish an agreed-upon vision from God."

One of the saddest verses in the Bible is 1 Samuel 3:1: "Now the young man Samuel was ministering to the LORD under Eli. And the word of the LORD was rare in those days; there was no frequent vision." There were times during Israel's history where people in general and leaders in particular were not hearing anything from the Lord and seldom was a vision from God received. I think we have a similar situation in churches today. Leaders are not hearing from God and there is no vision for the church in which they lead.

Dissatisfied

A leader is a person who is dissatisfied with the way things are. He has a God-given burden, a vision, and a call to see something different. He wants to see something change, to build a new future. He then begins to communicate what he thinks and where he wants to go. Because of the character and quality of his life, he is able to get others to join him. In the process of traveling toward this desired future, he sees that those traveling with him are being shepherded, developed, equipped, and empowered. This is appropriate because the word *lead* comes from an Old English root meaning "go, travel, guide."

To accomplish his tasks, he needs more than followers. He needs other leaders with certain gifts who share the same vision. You will see this pattern throughout the Bible, in the lives of people like Nehemiah, Moses, David, and Paul. They were people with God-given vision and they had the ability to enlist others to join them on their journeys.

So let's explore the topic of vision!

Visionary Leaders

A vision is a clear, challenging picture of the future of ministry as it can be and must be—*can be* because God has given it, and *must be* because he has placed the dream and the burden of this vision on the heart of a leader. Today, people are looking for a cause, a mountain to climb, and a leader to follow into new and exciting territory.

The key in motivating people to a cause is having a vision that is strong and compelling. There are many churches and organizations that have vision on paper but no vision in practice. A leader who has a vision possesses a clear picture of what he wants in the future. He carries a visual snapshot in his mental wallet.

As I have observed the leadership landscape, it seems those who occupy leadership positions fall into three categories:

- *The Administrator*. This is someone who accomplishes things through policy, guidelines, procedures, and regulations. He or she usually has the gift of administration and reaches a desired end by setting up procedure and policy.
- *The Lover*. This is usually someone with strong people skills who possesses the gifts of mercy, hospitality, and helps. He has a pastor's heart along with a strong love and concern for people's feelings and welfare.
- *The Visionary*. This individual is on a mission. They are gifted in motivating others, setting a direction, and creating excitement and a sense of adventure. They have a destination in mind and possess the ability to take others along on the journey.

There is certainly a place for the administrator and the lover, but the heart of this book and the cry of my heart is for more visionaries.

Vision Is Critically Essential

If you find yourself in a leadership role as pastor, elder, deacon, small-group leader, or ministry overseer, you need to have a dream, a vision from God. You also need the ability to get others to catch the vision as you travel toward your dream. If you are not a strong, natural visionary, you can still learn things to improve your ability to create a sense of vision.

On the other hand, if you find yourself in a leadership role and know that you are clearly not gifted or called to provide visionary leadership (revisit chapters 6 and 7 on calling and gifting), think in terms of recruiting or hiring a visionary team to whom you can defer. Don't let your ego or traditional job definitions get in the way.

Shortly after the completion of Disney World, someone said to Mike Vance, the director of Disney Studios, "Isn't it too bad that Walt Disney didn't live to see this?"

Vance replied, "He did see it—that's why it's here." That's vision in its purest sense.

I heard George Barna say, "Only 2 percent of pastors could articulate their vision for their churches." Is it any wonder that the present church in the United States is in decline? According to another source, "Eighty to eighty-five percent of American churches are either plateaued or dying with no revival in sight."[2] Could vision be the missing ingredient? I think the answer is a resounding yes.

Due to visionless ministry and churches, people are looking around. What will they find if they show up on your doorstep?

A little girl was sailing with her father from Long Beach to Catalina Island. It was an unusually clear day. In her excitement, she exclaimed, "Daddy, I can look farther than I can see!" Leaders with vision look beyond what is apparent to human eyes. They often see farther than others see and before others see.

Retired baseball manager Sparky Anderson said, "I've got my faults, but living in the past isn't one of them. There ain't no future in it." Vision is about the future.

There are three phases to seeing a vision fulfilled:

Fruitfulness

1. Developing the vision
2. Communicating the vision
3. Implementing the vision

Develop the Vision

Committees or boards don't develop vision. Vision comes from a visionary leader. I have not yet heard of a statue in a city park dedicated to a committee. Admittedly, communicating and implementing a vision should be a joint effort. However, in the Scriptures and in history, God usually births a vision in a leader's heart. Then that leader begins to speak about it and find others who will share that vision. Leaders get a dream from God when there is a deep dissatisfaction with what is and a deep desire for what could be. There is often restlessness about living with the status quo.

Many of today's successful ministries—including The Salvation Army, The Navigators, the Calvary Chapel movement, Campus Crusade for Christ, and Promise Keepers, to name a few—began when an individual got a glimpse of what could be. Who can adequately measure the impact Luther, Calvin, and Wesley had on church history? Time alone with God in solitude, reflection, and pondering the future often births and ignites vision.

Ask yourself what your ministry will look like as you reach the people in your area. The picture that begins to form in the mind and heart is the vision! It was Robert Kennedy who said, "Some see what is and ask 'why.' Others see what could be and ask 'why not.'"

Communicate the Vision

One of the primary roles of an effective leader for the twenty-first century is that of vision caster. This would include crafting and birthing a vision, then cultivating and clarifying the vision through creative communication. The leader doesn't do it alone, but should be the primary point person for this communication. I have yet to see any success when the leader delegates the responsibility for the caretaking of the vision to a board or committee. It is the leader's responsibility to ensure the vision is kept before the people.

Beware of these three things:

1. Lack of vision
2. A vision that is not clear
3. Communicating the vision inconsistently or ineffectively

There are those who have a vision but do not see the urgent need for keeping that vision alive and contagious in the hearts and minds of their followers. In a meeting I once heard Bill Hybels say, "If there is anything I have learned over the years, it is not to underestimate how often I need to rekindle the vision."

The vision needs to be repeated over and over in creative ways by various means and through a variety of people who are committed to it. People have short memories and need to be reminded of the big picture and how their part contributes to the whole. It is the leader's responsibility to set the pace, stirring up emotion and unleashing excitement about the future. Creative and continual communication from the leader first, and then from others, is the key to keeping the fire burning.

Implement the Vision

It is at this point that team effort pays off. Both communicating and implementing the vision is everybody's responsibility. The visionary leader leads the way and builds a team of excited players who are marching into the future with enthusiasm and high expectations.

How does the leader build a team of excited players? He does it through a process of strategic planning. This gives the vision wings. It is important to help people find their ministry niche.

The planning process can be described with words such as mobilizing, energizing, delegating, affirming, encouraging, collaborating, and evaluating. It is best done in the context of a team. According to George Cladis, "The key is a leadership team that lives the vision, breathes it, models it, tells its story every chance it gets, sleeps it, eats it, and otherwise calls people together around it."[3] A vision is usually birthed in isolation, but it is most effectively communicated and implemented in community.

A French Miracle

Walt Kallestad, senior pastor of Community of Joy Church in Glendale, Arizona, shares this inspiring story about vision.

A short time ago, I delivered four lectures at St. Nicholas Church in Strasbourg, France. In this church it is believed that John Calvin was a minister, Martin Luther preached, and Albert Schweitzer was the music minister. Wow—what a line-up! There had been people of great vision in this church. But now, the church doors were locked.

No one came any longer; only pigeons ever saw the inside. It happened because the vision or purpose for the church was lost. In 1992 the local bishop invited any pastor who was interested to submit a vision for this empty, historic church. One pastor was equal to the challenge. He stayed up all night writing down his vision.

He submitted it to the bishop, who eventually granted permission for the pastor to carry out his vision.

When I spoke later in that church, I was excited to see three-hundred to four-hundred people crammed into the building. Today that church has the largest attendance of any Lutheran church in France.[4]

Often a visionary leader with a burden and dream is the spark that starts the fire. A vision, although birthed in the heart of a single leader, must be communicated and carried out by many people. A truly effective leader operates in a network of supportive and complementary relationships.

Next, we will move on to the kinds of relationships a leader needs to develop in order to successfully reach the finish line and see the vision happen.

CHAPTER 11:

The Leader's Influence

"The key to successful leadership today is influence,
not authority."

KENNETH BLANCHARD

"Some people come into our lives and quietly go. Others stay a while and leave footprints on our hearts and we are never the same." As I mentioned earlier, this statement has had a very powerful impact on my life. As I sat in Sue Krenwinkle's office, I realized for the first time that I had a strong desire to influence others in a deep and lasting way—not inadvertently or casually, but proactively, intentionally, and strategically. I believe this desire needs to be the heartbeat of every true leader. Something deep down inside compels him or her to want to have influence in the lives of others.

The intentional influencing of others, found in my leadership definition, includes shepherding, developing, equipping, and empowering. These are some of the major aspects of what a leader does and how the people being led are influenced in order to reach mutually agreed upon objectives.

Teamwork Makes the Dream Work

A leader who lasts cannot fulfill God's purpose by himself. The notion of leading always encompasses others. The leader has a

God-given dream, and in order to see that dream fulfilled, he needs others with whom he can team. We live in a time when leadership is less of a one-person job and more of a team effort.

Be careful with whom you spend the bulk of your time. A leader influences many by investing in a few and letting those few influence the rest. In his book *The Tipping Point*, Malcolm Gladwell refers to the "law of the few."[1] He discusses the leverage a leader can have by investing in a few who can have great impact on others. There are certain people who can help you create change and forward progress because they will talk with and influence others.

Once these key influencers are identified, they can join the effort by becoming part of an inner circle, like the circle of influencers that both Jesus and Paul had. Your job then becomes one of investing in these key individuals. You will want to make sure that these key people are shepherded, developed, equipped, and empowered so that they are excited and believe deeply in the vision. They in turn will influence others.

Jethro's Solution

Much of what we see today and read about speaks to the necessity of leaders who are team players and team builders. The responsibilities required to see the vision fulfilled are spread within a team. It is impossible, unbiblical, and unwise for a leader, whether lead pastor, staff person, head of a ministry, or even a small-group leader, to go it alone. The story of Jethro and Moses in Exodus 18 should have forever settled the issue. Bill Easum, whom I mentioned earlier, says that a shift needs to take place. The lead pastor should see his flock as a few key staff and leaders, not the entire congregation.

All I have said thus far has been to encourage you to be a leader who is walking closely with the Lord, leading and managing yourself well, knowing who you are by clearly identifying your calling and gifts, and being a lifelong learner who is constantly growing. You lead others from the depths of who you are. The DNA of an organization, church, or group is often the extension of its leader. Who you are always precedes how you lead.

Followers don't do what leaders say as much as they do what leaders do. Modeling has much to do with Christlikeness—authenticity, genuineness, and the fruit of the Spirit. In Paul's first letter to the believers in Thessalonica, he says that he didn't merely give the gospel, but his own life as well, because they had become dear to him (1 Thess. 2:8). Leaders have their greatest influence by being up close and personal.

Howard Hendricks of Dallas Theological Seminary said, "You can impress people at a distance, but you can impact them only up close."[2] Life-on-life coaching, building close relationships, and genuinely caring for key people is the way to have lasting impact. This will enable you to influence many others. Those who have had the biggest influence on my life have been more than teachers or bosses. They have taken the next step to be my friend, coach, and cheerleader.

One of my early coaches, Warren Myers, was this kind of friend. He showed great concern for me and my family, praying regularly for us until the day he died in 2001. He encouraged me and was there for me. He modeled godly character through his life more than he taught through his lips.

Fruitfulness

A leader is a person who is on a journey and has the ability to attract others to join him on that journey. Because a leader's greatest assets are the people he influences, one of the real challenges in leadership is to figure out what kinds of people one should be involved with and what amount of time should be invested. The people with whom the leader spends time will determine the effectiveness of that leader. Certain people have great potential in helping us fulfill a vision, while other people can be the source of our biggest headaches and heartaches. For the remainder of this chapter, I want to focus on the kinds of people that leaders should spend time with and how to allocate that time in a strategic way so as to maximize their influence.

Proactive or Reactive

Prioritizing certain kinds of people to invest in is critical to leading well. Many church leaders, especially lead pastors, are reactive in deciding who gets their time, rather than proactive and strategic. This has to change! We need to think in terms of five different groups of people with whom we spend our time:

1. Resourceful people
2. Important people
3. Trainable people
4. Nice people
5. Draining people

After years of working with people in the above categories, Gordon MacDonald—author, speaker, and pastor—arrived at a startling conclusion:

I was making a serious mistake. Because the nice people were so pleasant to be with, and because the draining people requested so much time, I had little prime time left over for the resourceful and the trainable people. None of the latter two made the demands upon me that the first two did. And, I, because they made so few protests, left them alone as a rule because I thought I was where I was most needed; an error of great magnitude.[3]

I have personally learned much from Gordon's experience. I am slow and deliberate in agreeing to spend significant time with a person. The need is not the call. Just because someone has a need doesn't necessarily mean I am the one who must meet it.

Because of my purpose statement to "leave footprints in the hearts of God-hungry leaders," most of my time is spent with leaders who are hungry for more. Your purpose statement should help you decide with whom you invest time and how much time you invest.

One of the things that can torpedo a leader is spending large amounts of time with the wrong people. Our ability to reach our goals and achieve our God-given vision is dramatically affected by the people who populate our appointment calendars.

Highly Ineffective People

I wrote an article entitled "Seven Habits of Highly Ineffective Leaders," a satire based on Stephen Covey's book, *The Seven Habits of Highly Effective People*.[4] Here's the list:

1. They spend too much time managing and not enough time leading.

2. They spend too much time counseling the hurting people and not enough time developing the people with potential.
3. They spend too much time putting out fires and not enough time lighting fires.
4. They spend too much time doing and not enough time planning.
5. They spend too much time teaching the crowd and not enough time training the core.
6. They spend too much time doing it themselves and not enough time doing it through others.
7. They make too many decisions based on organizational politics and too few decisions based on biblical principles.

Notice in particular numbers 2, 5, and 6, which have to do with the kinds of people you spend time with. I say it again: the people you spend the majority of your time with can and will determine whether you are an effective or ineffective leader.

The fact is that many people in leadership roles gravitate toward hurting, draining, time-consuming people because they have a need to be needed. They want to help people, to be there for people. If a leader has strong mercy gifts, leading becomes more difficult. Simply put, if you need people, you can't lead people. There is an inability or lack of desire to make the tough calls, speak the truth, or do the hard things. Motivated by a fear of disappointing people, this inability will seriously hamper and work against your ability to lead.

Allocating Your Time Wisely

I have come to the conclusion that the average leaders will allocate their time in the following five areas:

1. Teaching and communicating
2. Counseling
3. Administering
4. Equipping and training others
5. Vision casting

As I have had opportunity to observe and invest in leaders over forty years, I have concluded that Christian leaders spend most of their time teaching, counseling, and administering. The two areas that are woefully shortchanged are vision casting and equipping/training.

We will deal with future leaders in the next chapter. We covered vision casting in the prior chapter. Let's focus here on investing time in resourceful and trainable people (growing disciples), some of whom will become future leaders.

Filling Your Calendar with the Right People

Why is so little time invested in the right kinds of people? The draining and nice people get all the prime time. The resourceful (those that infuse you with new perspective and energy) and the trainable (those you can equip) get the leftovers.

As a leader, I desperately need something that doesn't appear on any organization chart: the inclusion of resourceful people in my life. These are people who are coaches and encouragers. These are individuals who inspire me, lift me up, hold me accountable, motivate me, believe in me, confront me, and love me. Author John Gardner notes, "The leader needs a circle of associates who are willing to be both supportive and critical. Pity the leader who is caught between unloving critics and uncritical lovers."[5]

Fruitfulness

I am convinced that every leader needs, among resourceful people, at least one person of the same sex to whom she or he may be accountable. When we read of fallen and disgraced leaders, they are usually not accountable to anyone. I praise the Lord for Keith, my current accountability partner. Keith is not afraid to ask me the tough questions. We meet monthly. I have asked him to be in my face and in my life. He has saved my neck more than once, and I listen carefully to everything he says.

Accountability

As I am writing this chapter, a well-known pastor in Southern California has been removed from leadership due to moral and financial failure. This pastor believed that accountability was a waste of his time. "People lie and tell you what you want to hear," was what he said. It was OK with him if others on his large pastoral staff sought out accountability, but he saw it as a waste of time. Left alone, he fell, and now the church is picking up the pieces and searching for a new pastor. Countless lives have been negatively impacted, and the cause of Christ has been deeply hurt by his lack of leadership accountability.

If you and your leadership team are not careful, the vision will never fully materialize. There will be no intentional time with the hungry kinds of people you need to focus on in order to continue to make progress. I am not saying that the nice and the draining people are not valuable to God. I am saying that a leader simply cannot afford to spend most of his time with them. He needs to delegate that task to others, applying the principle of the early church found in Acts 6:1–4.

Watch Out for Counseling

I strongly encourage you to be intentional, prayerful, careful, and strategic regarding those with whom you spend your time. Be especially careful of using up all your "people hours" in counseling. Some pastors and leaders have gotten out of the counseling business altogether. If you are not careful, counseling can suck the life out of you. There will be nothing left for your spouse, family, and trainable or resourceful people. Counseling is a big issue for many leaders and is a hotly debated topic.

I see a trend of effective leaders bringing counselors onto their staffs or referring out counseling needs. The only ones they counsel are the growing disciples and future leaders. A heavy counseling load panders to the need to be needed and can sink your leadership ship faster than anything.

I once read of Peter Drucker's meetings with a banker. The meetings were always set for ninety minutes. The banker was always on time and would usher him into his office. At the end of the ninety minutes, he would rise like clockwork and usher him out.

It occurred to Drucker that they were never interrupted and that their times together were always ninety minutes in length. When he asked the banker about this, he was told that he had discovered that a ninety-minute time frame was his optimal working time. He could keep focused and stay on task for that length of time, so he built his day around ninety-minute blocks. He would work for ninety minutes, take a break, talk with his secretary, and then work for another ninety minutes.

Drucker mentioned to the banker that they were never interrupted during their meetings, which was unusual in his experience with a man of his responsibilities. The banker remarked that there were only two people who had permission to barge in on his ninety-minute working blocks of time: the president of the United States and the banker's wife. The banker remarked, "The president has never bothered to call, and my wife knows better." Here is a man who had the discipline and the vision to make sure he was getting time with the right people. He was a man who was proactive and not reactive with regard to who received his time and attention.

It has been said that if you don't plan your life, someone will plan it for you. Usually the nice and draining people will take care of that. This will result in your not growing into the leader you were meant to be, because you have no time for resourceful people, trainable people, or future leaders. You'll fail to exercise one of your primary responsibilities as a leader.

I strongly suggest that you arrange your life, time, and weekly schedule to be able to invest in trainable people; growing, hungry, teachable disciples; and potential leaders. Make sure that growing disciples are motivated and encouraged to grow in the basics of Christian living. See that they receive more than a sermon on Sunday morning, and make sure that they are involved in small groups and discipled by mature believers.

There is an enormous emphasis placed on teaching large groups and entirely too little emphasis on small groups and life-on-life discipleship. Much material is available for helping young believers grow into fully devoted followers, so I won't go into more detail here. Suffice it to say, a leader needs to spend the largest chunk of his "people hours" meeting with disciples hungry for training, not counseling with draining people.

Among these growing disciples will be some who clearly have leadership gifts. These future leaders should get your prime time. This is the biggest missing piece. I meet very few Christian leaders who are intentionally and strategically investing in future leaders.

A New Spin on the Need for Workers

Bobby Clinton says:

> If the Lord was to make a statement to us, looking not only at the leadership gap but also at the present leaders, he might rephrase Matthew 9:36–38 as follows: "When he saw the leaders, he was filled with dismay, because so many quit, so many were set aside, and so many were plateaued and directionless. They had lost their zest for leading. They had no clear philosophy or direction in their leadership. They were leaderless leaders. Then he said to his disciples, 'The harvest is plentiful, but the leaders with clear direction are few. Ask the Lord of the harvest that he will send forth knowledgeable, discerning and direction-oriented leader-laborers into his harvest.'"[6]

We must learn to take time from other important and pressing needs to impact the next generation of leaders.

Let's deal next with the leader who develops leaders.

CHAPTER 12

The Leader's Legacy

"I start with the premise that the function of leadership is to produce more leaders, not more followers."

RALPH NADER

Today, the crying need is for more leaders. To grow by *addition*, you recruit more followers. To grow by *multiplication*, you add more leaders. Who will discover, develop, and deploy them? The top priority of a leader must be to invest in future leaders. John Maxwell says that it takes one to know one, to show one, and to grow one. Materials, books, seminars, and conferences won't make leaders. Leaders make leaders. When the apostle Paul was giving instructions to Timothy and Titus, he made it clear that it was their job to select leaders, and gave them a list of qualifications on which to base their selection (1 Timothy 3; Titus 1).

The reason there is a dearth of leaders today is that too little of the average leader's time is focused on leadership development. Only when current leaders become leader-makers will our organizations, churches, and groups begin to develop the numbers and kinds of leaders needed to make a significant impact for Jesus. The single greatest way to impact an organization is to focus on leadership development.

Investing in the Next Generation of Leaders

We can think back with a smile as we recall Moses' encounter with his wise father-in-law in Exodus 18. Jethro was perplexed about why all the people were lined up to talk with Moses, the leader. His wise counsel to Moses—to develop other leaders to carry the responsibility with him—is still relevant today.

The cry today is, "We need more leaders!" But the attitude, it would appear, is to hope and pray that someday, all of a sudden, godly, motivated, equipped leaders will magically appear, ready to roll. The reality, however, is that leaders need to commit a much greater portion of their time to influencing future leaders.

When the need is so apparent and pressing, why do leaders fail to spend significant time developing additional leaders? Here are a few reasons that keep them from it.

- *Insecurity.* The thought of having someone around who might be better at aspects of leading than they are—let alone furthering the development of such people—is too much for them to handle. I am reminded of the memo from a company president that said, "Search the organization for an alert, aggressive, gifted young man who could someday step into my shoes. And when you find him, fire him!"
- *Low Priority.* Developing leaders is not a high value and, therefore, is not intentionally pursued.
- *Not Trained.* If a leader has never been discipled, coached, or trained, it is unlikely he will have the skills or motivation to develop leadership abilities in others.
- *Lack of Relational Skills.* Some leaders are task oriented and extremely impersonal. They fear getting close to people. They aren't willing to be open, transparent, or vulnerable— all essential qualities for developing new leaders.

Dallas Seminary professor Aubrey Malphurs put it well when he said, "Ministry must not be primarily equated with the communication of biblical truth from a pulpit in a sanctuary or a podium in a classroom. The pastor needs to be a leader and a coach of leaders as well as a preacher. Future pastors graduate not knowing how to recruit and train leaders."[1]

It is Aubrey's belief that we need a new paradigm for the lead pastoral role to help accomplish the Great Commission in the twenty-first century. He suggests three key responsibilities:[2]

1. Primary communicator
2. Developer of present and potential leadership
3. Primary vision caster

Getting Started in the Investment Business

Here are some suggestions to enable all leaders to begin to develop new leaders:

1. Make leadership development a priority and let your goals, schedule, and time with people show it.
2. Begin to pray for God-hungry, potential leaders. Ask the Lord to give you the eyes to see them and the courage to approach them.
3. Select a few to start with. Look for teachable, available, and growing disciples who might already be leading (or have experience leading) at school or in the marketplace. These are the ones you can take to the next level.
4. Assemble subject material to cover under the following three major categories: Character (being), Caring (relating), and Competence (doing). To get the ball rolling, here are a few suggested topics:

Fruitfulness

Character	Caring	Competence
Faithfulness	Love	Public communication
Honesty	Listening	Leading a small group
Teachability	Vulnerability	Mentoring others
Joy	Team playing	Sharing the gospel
Humility	Flexibility	Leading a meeting
		Decision making

Share your own journey, your successes, and your failures as you cover these areas. You can use resources, such as books, CDs, articles, and Web sites. You can also encourage them to get personal time with other leaders you know who have specific gifts and experiences that can be of help to your leaders in training.

5. Individualize your plan. Devise your plan according to the experience and maturity of the potential leader. You won't work with every leader the same way. Paul says in 1 Thessalonians 2:11–12, "For you know how, like a father with his children, we exhorted each one of you . . . " One commentator says, "how we dealt with each one of you personally like a Father with his own children" (PHILLIPS). Just as each child is different, so is each leader.

6. Give added responsibilities incrementally as each one becomes ready.

7. Continue to encourage and express belief in them. I have never met a person who complained that they were encouraged too much. Try to catch your leaders doing something right, not doing something wrong.

In working to develop a potential leader, start by directing them in some responsibility. As they get into it, they need coaching. Make your own experience available to them and help them as they have questions. Then, as you gradually wean them from your close supervision, they need you to be supportive. The last stage is the *delegation* of tasks from you to the developing leader, and then, finally, they are on their own.[3]

Many leaders start at stage one by giving a job or task to a new leader, then take their hands off and move to stage four, releasing them too quickly to be on their own. I am increasingly learning how to coach in stage two and support in stage three. Moving too quickly from one to four is not delegating but abdicating. Without coaching and support, this process doesn't work for growing leaders. It takes time and careful planning to develop leaders (another reason why leadership development is not a priority for a lot of leaders).

Your greatest legacy as a leader is to leave other leaders in your wake that can carry on after you are no longer there. You are a leader who has experienced what a leader faces in your specific role. Make it your priority and goal to pour your life into future leaders!

Get Started . . . Don't Wait Another Minute

The leader's greatest calling and most significant long-term contribution is to recruit and train other leaders. Moses had Joshua, Elijah had Elisha, Paul had Timothy, and Jesus had the Twelve. I implore you as a leader to take who you are, along with the things you've learned and experienced, and invest in other potential leaders and influencers on a personal level. Paul told Timothy to take what he had heard and invest it in faithful men who would train others (2 Tim. 2:2); reflect on the people around you, identify potential leaders, and start investing in them.

The incredible shortage of leaders today adds fuel to my motivation for investing a majority of time in "leaving footprints in the hearts of God-hungry leaders who multiply." You will never be an effective leader by creating only followers. Leader, where are your future leaders? Where are the leaders who can "bear the burden of the people with you, so that you may not bear it yourself alone" (Num. 11:17)?

Thinking Things Through

Part Three

1. Do you have a clear vision from the Lord? Do significant influencers share that vision with you?
2. Where are you in the process of developing, communicating, and implementing that God-given vision?
3. How are you spending time with the right people? What adjustments do you need to make? As you look at your schedule, what types of people populate it?
4. Name the future leaders in whom you are currently investing. What is your game plan for each of them?

Epilogue

The life of a leader is like a race. We have been discussing this throughout the book. If you are to be among the leaders who last, it will take time and effort both to get ready and to run the race. It takes adequate preparation, constant attention, and steady pacing to finish well. It's not a matter of running an individual race. Rather, it's more like a relay race, a team effort. You want to finish well, but not by yourself. The successful leader is a humble, God-dependent, team-playing servant of God with the vision, calling, gifts, and abilities to bring others into the race.

By 7:00 p.m. on October 20, 1968, at the Mexico City Olympics Stadium, it was beginning to darken, and the weather had cooled. The last of the Olympic marathon runners were being assisted away to first-aid stations. Over an hour earlier, Mamo Waldi of Ethiopia had charged across the finish line, winning the 26-mile, 385-yard race, looking as strong and as vigorous as when he started. As the last few thousand spectators began preparing to leave, they heard police sirens and whistles blaring through the gate. Their attention turned to that gate. A sole figure, wearing the colors of Tanzania, came limping into the stadium. His name was John Steven Aquari. He was the last man to finish the marathon. His leg was bandaged and bloody, due to a bad fall he had taken early in the race.

Now it was all he could do to limp his way around the track. The crowd stood and applauded as he completed that last lap.

When he finally crossed the finish line, one man dared to ask the question all were wondering, "You are badly injured. Why didn't you quit? Why didn't you give up?"

Aquari answered with quiet dignity, "My country did not send me seven thousand miles to start this race, but to finish it."

My fellow leader, Jesus did not call, equip, and put you into a leadership role to have you start and then quit, plateau, or be disqualified. He called you to finish the race, and finish it well. It is my prayer that you, with his help, will be a leader who lasts, a leader who will hear those wonderful words as you hit the ribbon in full stride: "Well done, good and faithful servant."

Notes

Prologue
1. Knute Larson, *The Great Human Race* (Wheaton, IL: Victor Books, 1987).

Introduction
1. J. Robert Clinton, *The Making of a Leader* (Colorado Springs, CO: NavPress, 1988).

Chapter One: The Leader's Power
1. Adapted from an interview with John Ortberg, "Holy Tension," *Leadership Journal* (Winter 2004).
2. This material was adapted from an InterVarsity newsletter.

Chapter Two: The Leader's Purpose
1. Os Guinness, *The Call* (Nashville, TN: Word, 1998), 203.
2. J. Robert Clinton, *The Making of a Leader* (Colorado Springs, CO: NavPress, 1988).
3. Laurie Beth Jones, *The Path: Creating Your Mission Statement for Work and Life* (New York: Hyperion, 1996).
4. Os Guinness, *The Call*, 1.
5. "Find What You Were Born to Do," *Current Thoughts & Trends* 19, no. 1 (January 2003): 5 (excerpted from Pythia Peay, "Who Are You Really," *Utne Reader* [November/December 2002]: 59–62).

Chapter Three: The Leader's Passion
1. Bill Bradley, *Values of the Game* (New York: Artisan, 1998), 23.
2. Nigel Hamilton, *JFK, Reckless Youth* (New York: Random House, 1992), 443.
3. Transcribed from a talk given by John Maxwell on *The Power of Passion*. See http://www.johnmaxwell.com.

4. Charles R. Swindoll, *The Quest for Character* (Portland, OR: Multnomah Press, 1987), 166.

Chapter Four: The Leader's Priorities

1. James C. Collins, *Good to Great: Why Some Companies Make the Leap—and Others Don't* (New York: HarperBusiness, 2001), 139.
2. Charles Edward Jones, *Life Is Tremendous* (Wheaton, IL: Tyndale House Publishers, 1968), 42–44.

Chapter Five: The Leader's Pacing

1. Wayne Muller, "Remember the Sabbath," *The Desert Sun*, April 4, 1999.

Chapter Six: The Leader's Calling

1. Oswald Chambers, *My Utmost for His Highest*, August 5.
2. Eddie Gibbs, *ChurchNext: Quantum Changes in How We Do Ministry* (Downers Grove, IL: InterVarsity Press, 2000), 101.
3. Michael Ross, *The Christian Times*, May 2001. See http://www.christian examiner.com/Pages/Archive.html.

Chapter Eight: The Leader's Character

1. Bill Thrall, Bruce McNicol, and Ken McElrath, *The Ascent of a Leader: How Ordinary Relationships Develop Extraordinary Character and Influence* (San Francisco, CA: Jossey-Bass, 1999).
2. James C. Hunter, *The World's Most Powerful Leadership Principle: How to Become a Servant Leader* (Colorado Springs: WaterBrook Press, 2004), 141.
3. James M. Kouzes and Barry Z. Posner, *The Leadership Challenge: How to Get Extraordinary Things Done in Organizations* (San Francisco, CA: Jossey-Bass, 1987), 16.
4. John R. Wooden and Jack Tobin, *They Call Me Coach* (Waco, TX: Word Books, 1972), 62.
5. John C. Maxwell, *The 21 Indispensable Qualities of a Leader: Becoming the Person Others Will Want to Follow* (Nashville: Thomas Nelson, 1999).

Chapter Nine: The Leader's Growth

1. Tom Peters, "The New World of Work: Free at Last!?" May 2000, http://www.tompeters.com/resources/obs_entries.php?date=200005.
2. Paul D. Stanley and J. Robert Clinton, *Connecting: The Mentoring Relationships You Need to Succeed in Life* (Colorado Springs, CO: NavPress, 1992).

3. Thomas C. Bandy, "Breaking Free from Control," *Net Results* 23, no. 8 (September 2002): 12.
4. Melissa Chessher, "Executive 2000," *American Way Magazine*, http://www.crupi.com/amerway.html.
5. Howard G. Hendricks, *Teaching to Change Lives* (Sisters, OR: Multnomah, 1987), 14.

Chapter Ten: The Leader's Vision

1. Robert K. Greenleaf, *Servant Leadership* (Mahwah, NJ: Paulist Press, 1977), 16.
2. Aubrey Malphurs, *Developing a Vision for Ministry in the 21st Century* (Grand Rapids, MI: Baker, 1992), 13.
3. George Cladis, *Leading the Team-Based Church: How Pastors and Church Staffs Can Grow Together into a Powerful Fellowship of Leaders* (San Francisco, CA: Jossey-Bass, 1999), 56.
4. Walther P. Kallestad, *The Everyday Anytime Guide to Christian Leadership* (Minneapolis: Augsburg, 1994), 25.

Chapter Eleven: The Leader's Influence

1. Malcolm Gladwell, *The Tipping Point: How Little Things Can Make a Big Difference* (Boston: Little, Brown, 2000).
2. Howard G. Hendricks, *Teaching to Change Lives* (Portland, OR: Multnomah/Walk thru the Bible Ministries, 1987), 117.
3. Gordon MacDonald, *Restoring Your Spiritual Passion* (Nashville: Oliver-Nelson Books, 1986), 88.
4. Stephen R. Covey, *The Seven Habits of Highly Effective People* (New York: Simon and Schuster, 1989).
5. John W. Gardner, *On Leadership* (New York: Free Press, 1990), 135.
6. J. Robert Clinton, *The Making of a Leader* (Colorado Springs, CO: NavPress, 1988), 202–3.

Chapter Twelve: The Leader's Legacy

1. Aubrey Malphurs, *Ministry Nuts and Bolts: What They Don't Teach Pastors in Seminary* (Grand Rapids, MI: Kregel, 1997), 12.
2. Aubrey Malphurs, *Developing a Vision for Ministry in the 21st Century* (Grand Rapids, MI: Baker, 1992), 85.
3. Kenneth H. Blanchard, John P. Carlos, and W. Alan Randolph, *The Three Keys to Empowerment: Release the Power within People for Astonishing Results* (San Francisco, CA: Berrett-Koehler, 1999).

General Index

RE:LIT

Resurgence Literature (Re:Lit) is a ministry of the Resurgence. At www.theResurgence.com you will find free theological resources in blog, audio, video, and print forms, along with information on forthcoming conferences, to help Christians contend for and contextualize Jesus' gospel. At www.ReLit.org you will also find the full lineup of Resurgence books for sale. The elders of Mars Hill Church have generously agreed to support Resurgence and the Acts 29 Church Planting Network in an effort to serve the entire church.

FOR MORE RESOURCES

Re:Lit – www.ReLit.org
Resurgence – www.theResurgence.com
Re:Sound – www.resound.org
Mars Hill Church – www.marshillchurch.org
Acts 29 – www.acts29network.org

Dave Kraft's Blog – http://davekraft.org
Dave Kraft's E-mail – dave@marshillchurch.org